# Approaches
# to Insanity

Although the book's focus is the critical examination of the theories of schizophrenia, a job that is done with rare freshness, conciseness, and critical appreciation of the metatheoretical underpinnings of each of the major approaches, its ultimate aim is to persuade the reader towards a new approach to the general problem of deviance attribution (termed "ascription" by the author). Its emphasis on attribution theory, deviance and on a socio-cultural approach to the understanding of cognition involved in attribution (here termed "ethnomethodology") makes this of contemporary interest to social scientists.

# Approaches to Insanity

*A Philosophical
& Sociological Study*

JEFF COULTER

A Halsted Press Book

JOHN WILEY & SONS
New York

Published in the USA by Halsted Press, a Division of John Wiley and Sons Inc. New York.

ISBN 0 470–17740–3
LCCC No. 73–19679

Printed in Britain at The Pitman Press, Bath

# Contents

# Dedications & Acknowledgements

*I should like to thank my wife, Lena, for enduring my extra-curricular academic obsessions over the months during which this work was undertaken and revised, for her continuing critical contributions, and for her inspiration. I should also like to register my thanks to my parents whose many sacrifices have enabled me to pursue learning at two universities. To my wife and parents this work is most affectionately dedicated.*

*On the formal, academic level I have to thank Dr Robert Ferguson, former Consultant Psychiatrist and now Senior Lecturer in Sociology, University of Salford; Dr. W. W. Sharrock, Lecturer in Sociology, University of Manchester (currently Visiting Assistant Professor, University of British Columbia, Canada); Dr Hassan Taufiq, Consultant Psychiatrist, Khartoum Hospital Psychiatric Section, Sudan; and the staff of a large Mental Welfare Department in the United Kingdom who kindly facilitated my research and put up with many niggling questions. None of these colleagues and associates will necessarily agree with the theses defended in this work, but the impetus to write it derived in large measure from discussions with them.*

# Introductory Remarks

This book is neither a textbook in psychopathology, nor an attempt to popularise that subject. Its purpose is to engage in a debate which currently straddles several disciplines whose theoreticians and researchers have been involved in work on 'the schizophrenias': psychology, sociology and biology. The inverted commas around the term schizophrenias point up the present controversies and disputes that pervade the areas of research to be examined in this work.

I have chosen to treat the available materials *selectively*, picking out what I consider to be the best work representing the various styles of theorizing and research. For much of what I have omitted, I have to claim that the recurrent methodological and conceptual troubles isolated here can be found there also. Essentially, what follows is a series of related chapters grouped into two parts, the first focusing upon the substantive literature on 'schizophrenia', and the second establishing a complete break from such an orientation and focusing instead on the natural logic of insanity ascription. The disjunction is perhaps most adequately summarised by stating that the first section deals with what somaticists, psychologists, sociologists and phenomenologists have made of 'the schizophrenias', whilst the second section leaves that focus behind and the second-order psychiatric taxonomy along with it, seeking to deal with Anyman's ways of construing insanity, where insanity is taken as a first-order ascriptive label equivalent to 'madness', 'mental disorder' and so on. The reasons for this disjunction will, I hope, become clear as we proceed.

The hopes I have for a lenient hearing derive in part from the attempt to cover a rather wide range of issues which I believe are interrelated in terms of my argument, and in part from my belief that the human sciences cannot be considered to have attained that stage of intellectual development where the boundaries of specialism and esoteric knowledge are tightly drawn.

In this work, I have drawn a persistent distinction between *psychiatry*, understood as an irremediably practical and pragmatic affair, and *psychopathology*, understood as a theoretical enterprize that aims to rationalize the experiences with insane members of a community in scientific terms. The hiatus which I describe between these two fields of work obviates the necessity for much discussion of therapy and treatment schedules (in which domain I am not a competent traveller). It is quite clear that psychopharmacologists have got on with their work independently of any advances in aetiological theorizing in the area of the schizophrenias—had we waited for unequivocal explanatory models from the aetiological theorists before we developed our psychotropic drugs and ECT schedules, we should still be without any physical methods of treatment for mental patients. Some might argue that this would have been no bad thing. But such an argument lies outside the scope of consideration in this work.

The architecture of this book reflects the logic of my own understanding of the salient issues, and should not be read as reflecting a chronological development either in psychopathology itself or in the debates in it and about it. Some of the questions addressed include :

What kind of thing is 'schizophrenia'?

Can we speak of schizophrenia as a disease?

What does it mean to suggest that 'the schizophrenias are inherited'?

Do psychiatrists concur as to the nature of schizophrenia both in particular cases and in general?

Can social events or processes *cause* schizophrenia, in any of its modalities?

Is it possible to decipher or render intelligible the communicative activities of insane people?

Are there any non-evaluative rules for making psychiatric diagnoses?

What is the role of 'culture' in ascriptions of mental disorder?

Is 'schizophrenia' only a convenient label?

How is our commonsense knowledge of mental states and functioning invoked with respect to ascriptions of and dealings with insanity?

It is clear that much has already been said in answer to these questions; the literature on mental disorders is quite out of proportion to the adequacy of our knowledge about them. What I hoped to achieve here was a clarification of some of the conceptual and substantive issues that seem, time and time again, to recur and frustrate the development of satisfactory approaches to insanity. The sort of answers that are provided in the available literature so frequently invoke the rhetoric of causation and provide the substance of 'approximations' only. This in itself has stimulated a resurgence of concern with the logical status of causal and quasi-causal explanations in the non-biological human sciences, and I take this up in various ways in the text. Again, a recurrent problem has been the polymorphous character of the concepts used by psychiatrists and others to ratify commonsense ascriptions of insanity, and their resistance to meaningful operationalization. My own response to such concerns draws heavily on the ideas of contemporary analytic philosophy and the work of Harold Garfinkel on the natural logic of situated practical action and practical reasoning. I begin with a discussion of the medical model or disease nosology of the schizophrenias, and conclude with some remarks on cognition as a moral order. If my conclusions satisfy no one but myself, I hope at least to share my journey to their construction with the reader.

*Jeff Coulter*
*Manchester, October 1972*

# PART ONE

*Theoretical Issues in Formal Psychopathology*

# CHAPTER ONE

# Schizophrenia as a Disease

My interest in opening an extended discussion of the disease theory of the schizophrenias is a theoretical, not a practical, one. I have no general prescriptions to offer for changes in contemporary psychiatric practice, and no political programme for transformations in the legal and administrative frameworks within which psychiatrists and psychiatric social workers operate. These issues are not my concern here. What I want to do is to consider the *status* of the major explanatory and research-guiding paradigm[1] within psychopathology in conceptual and methodological terms.

I am doubtful whether our discussion would be facilitated by the provision of any preliminary definition of 'disease'. Neither are etymological remarks in order at this point. Why should we think that those phenomena to which we intelligibly refer with the word 'disease' should manifest invariant, common properties that we could codify neatly into a list or a definition? Most of the attempts at definition seem to produce only woolly generalities that hardly serve us as heuristic devices : take David Mechanic's formulation, 'a disease is some deviation from normal functioning which has undesirable consequences, because it produces personal discomfort or adversely affects the individual's future health status,'[2] or David P. Ausubel's similar one, 'any marked deviation, physical, mental or behavioural, from normally desirable standards of structural and functional integrity'.[3] Mechanic's definition would enable us to call being beaten up in the street a 'disease', along with a range of other social problems, whilst Ausubel's could include a bad headache, a fit of rage or a knife in the ribs under its auspices.

It seems to me that much of the ink that is wasted in constructing definitions of 'disease' derives from the attempt in psychopathology to rationalize the use of the medical nosology. Instead of 'insanity', 'madness' or 'mental disorder,' we read of people suffering from

3

mental illnesses or mental diseases. (We find the former as well, but the tendency is to consider those terms as prejorative by contrast to the objective character of the medical terms). Yet the burden of this chapter is not only to demonstrate that there is no equivalent in insanity to something like the basic lesion of glucose intolerance characterising diabetes mellitus, but that the range of medical metaphors used in psychopathology is unwarranted for *theoretical* purposes. This is not to deny the usefulness of the medical nosology in practical psychiatry for such conditions as general paresis, neuro-syphilitic dementia or Gjessing's syndrome. What is in question is the foundation of the parallelism between physiological and psychosocial 'symptoms' *tout court*.

The 'symptoms' of the 'schizophrenias' are not bodily complaints, nor are they identified through the judicious use of the props of medical technology (blood-pressure gauges, thermometers, electro-encephalographs, X-rays, whitecell counts, galvanometers etc.), even though medical apparatus comes into play in treatment schedules. Rather, the 'symptoms' are framed as the result of the application of a disease model to people's talk and conduct, their beliefs and com-municated experiences. Either such talk and conduct are understood as *evidence of* some disease process that underlies them, or they are treated as the illness *itself;* in the former case, reasearch is supposed to uncover the organic pathology whilst in the latter case the termi-nology of disease and illness is used as a form of social castigation wherein one is literally seen to be 'sick in mind'. In this chapter, I am concerned solely with the former perspective, since there is little that I or anybody else can do with the latter—if someone wishes to use a vocabulary of metaphors for purposes of labelling mental patients, that is their business and not the business of science.

The diversity of activities, beliefs and communicated experiences that are presented by people diagnosed as 'schizophrenic' (in any of its subtypes) resists distillation into a formula or generalized descrip-tion. As 'schizophrenia' has no fixed attributes, any attempt at generalized description is bound to produce only a synecdochal (that is, partial) representation of the cases routinely subsumed to it in psychiatric practice. Symptomatological texts, with their clinical profiles, attempt to unify the heterogeneous presentations of diagnosed people into sets and subsets for purposes of practical psychiatric train-ing, but this sometimes reinforces the unwarranted impression that we are dealing with 'conditions' whose parameters are more or less determinate. The disease model of the schizophrenias is *essentially* predicated upon the assumption that such reifications are permissible for *theoretical* purposes. However, the practical application of psychiatric labels is a pragmatic affair, and there is no explicit code with which to work since no precise, reliable operational descriptions of mental illness or mental health are available[4] or even possible. Whatever diagnostic categories *are* employed in practice is relative to the province of therapeutic specialism on the part of a clinician, and for many only the grossest idea of what might be the matter with a person is sufficient to enable them to arrive at accountable decisions on treatment scheduling.[5] Somatotherapists using psychotropic drugs such as the phenothiazines for psychotics or monoamine oxidase inhibitors for acute depressives rarely require to traffic in the terminology of the sub-types ('simple', 'chronic', 'paranoid' etc), whilst no particularly refined classifications are necessary for the use of electroplexies or electro-convulsive therapy, since it is not known exactly what occurs in people who undergo them apart from a general tendency for many of them to lose their depressions at least temporarily.

In effect, then, ascriptions of 'schizophrenia,' lacking any uniformly interpretable indicators for diagnosis, do not function like ascriptions of physical ailments. They are not arrived at in the same kind of way, and they do not carry any clear latitudes of symptomatological or therapeutic information. For a reader or researcher, being informed that 'X' was diagnosed as a 'schizophrenic' and no more, is to be given far less informational content than being told that 'X' was diagnosed as suffering from pneumonia. Researchers in psychopathology, therefore, if they use the pre-established diagnoses of professional clinicians to generate their sample populations, must rely upon the tacit knowledge of their scientific readership in extreme measure to establish some correspondence between their research descriptions and the phenomena researched.[6] When replications are attempted, this issue becomes critical. As D. Bannister has pointed out in his important paper on the logic of research programmes in psychopathology into the schizophrenias,[7] the term 'schizophrenia' has tended to function as an *omnibus* category, an overarching classificatory concept covering such diverse features as flatness of affect, syntactic distortion, delirious elation, grandiose yet articulate belief systems and hallucinatory experiences in various combinations. For this reason, there can be little genuine research continuity into aetiology or socio-economic correlates when diagnosticians (who alone are accorded the right of clinical judgement) have such an array to choose from for the application of the omnibus term. One clinician, confronted with a subject presenting what he judges to be flatness of affect and syntactic distortion can diagnose schizophrenia, whilst another clinician (or the same one at some other time) confronted with a subject manifesting hallucinatory experiences, whilst carefully explaining that he is in fact Christ returned from the Kingdom of Heaven, can bestow the same label of schizophrenia upon him. Since the diagnostic labels provide no specificity of informational content usable to a researcher who aims at generality in his studies (aetiological or epidemiological), it becomes apparent that nomothetic work cannot adequately be predicated upon the practical assessments of working clinicians. If the psychopathologist's sample population is produced on the basis of such practical and pragmatic assessments, the result is a series of diverse and unrelated studies with a plethora of incongruent dimensions grouped together under the same auspices.

In confronting the problem of the context-specificity of insanity ascriptions and associated research programmes, we are doing more than reasserting the existence of the well-known hiatus between the logic-in-use of researchers and the reconstructed logic of their research descriptions.[8] We are indicating an *irremediable* constraint on all such research. Remedial treatments have included work on diagnostic reliability and attempts to rectify divergencies that appear. I want to look at this approach briefly before moving on to more substantive concerns.

In the social and behavioural sciences, where instrumentation is largely absent (except in areas such as the psychology of perception and physiological psychology), and where literal measurement of cultural data is largely ruled out by virtue of the nature of such data, work on 'construct validity' has been proposed and employed as a method for testing the levels of concordance and intersubjective agreement on the referential application of some technical construct. A basic postulate of most of this work is that transpersonal replicability of construct application establishes some warrant for the 'objectivity' of the judgements that can be made with its use. In psychopathology, tests of diagnostic reliability take the form of construct validity tests on items in the psychiatric vocabulary. Clinicians are given clinical profiles on mental patients, already diagnosed by other clinicians elsewhere, and are asked to read them and then make a diagnosis applicable to them; or, they are asked to watch films in which patients are displaying their problematic talk and conduct and again asked to select an appropriate diagnostic label. They are neither allowed to confer with others nor are they permitted anything other than the information transmitted to them in the profiles or on the films. In this way, the concordance rates (and hence, the 'construct validity' or otherwise) of the diagnostic categories are rated. However, the measures of concordance do not in themselves stipulate at what point a level of 'adequacy' of construct objectivity has been attained—that is itself a judgemental process. Such tests, in fact, tell us nothing more and nothing less than the ability of participants to make discriminations with a particular item in the psychiatric vocabulary at a certain level of consistency over the course of the testing periods. B. A. Maher has pointed out that such tests in psychopathology have rarely specified the base rates for particular diagnoses amongst the clinicians taking part, so we can have no method of determining whether the concordances obtained reflect more than a chance consistency.[9] If one clinician diagnoses schizophrenia for 80% of all his cases and the same percentage is found in the diagnoses of the second clinician, both working in normal psychiatric practice, then they will agree on a chance basis 64% of the time. Moreover, concordance rates obtained from these experiments cannot indicate anything further—we are still in the dark about the level of routinization of recognition practices in ordinary psychiatric work. As Wootton,[10] Laing,[11] and Szasz[12] have remarked, in their different ways, psychiatric diagnostic procedures are fundamentally *evaluative,* and attempts to 'scientize' the practical, everyday pragmatics of this state of affairs cannot succeed. We find that the actual results of some reliability studies demonstrate rather wide variations in psychiatric evaluations. Arnoff,[13] in an early study of this genre, found that three psychiatrists agreed in only 20% of their cases and had a majority agreement in only 48%. Beck,[14] Zubin,[15] Kreitman and his colleagues,[16] Zigler and Phillips,[17] Freudenberg and Robertson,[18] Sandifer and his colleagues,[19] and, writing up their results in 1969, Katz and his colleagues,[20] all make substantially the same point : the system of classifying what are considered to be mental illnesses cannot be used to any appreciable level of intersubjective consistency. Even with respect to the placing of persons within such gross categories as psychotic and neurotic, considerable disagreements arise in the context of these tests.

It is as well to interpolate some comments about practical psychiatry here. The normative basis of the psychiatric enterprise and its inability to generate high levels of diagnostic concordances with its taxonomy of illnesses is not being portrayed as some kind of 'fault' in psychiatry itself. Diagnostic work in psychiatry is conducted for practical purposes of hospitalisation and treatment in line with the standards of practice in any particular culture : diagnoses are bases for inference and action, not attempts at literal measurement of phenomena. However, psychopathology has tended to function in research terms with the aid of clinical diagnoses, as we have noted, and this would seem to imply that the 'phenomena' being researched are unambiguously discriminable and literally describable—after all, psychopathology has longstanding claims to the mantle of science. If the constructs with which psychopathology operates do not enable its researchers to generate work in accordance with the scientific rationalities as, for example, inventoried by Garfinkel,[21] then problems are bound to arise with respect to its claims.

Having perhaps laboriously stated some of the constraints on psychiatric research (research conducted within orthodox psychopathology), the problem arises as to what we can make of its products. The disease model of the schizophrenias (and other 'functional' mental 'illnesses') leads the researcher to assimilate the myriad of incomprehensible acts and utterances of insane people into the only explanatory framework which has traditionally had bestowed upon it the sanctity of 'science' : the physicalist framework. Thomas Szasz[22] has argued forcefully against the use of this framework, as have British 'anti-psychiatrists' such as David Cooper;[23] but their arguments have largely been directed at the morality of psychiatric *practice* and the politics of the psychiatrist-patient relationship. As such, they are beyond our scope and interest. Nonetheless, common to both is the insistence that statements such as Kolle's, that all mental disorders are states determined by nature,[24] are totally misconceived. In other words, they deny the existence of biogenetic aetiological agencies as causal antecedents to schizophrenic, or so-called schizophrenic, beliefs and conduct. The psychopathologist interested in biochemical models of insanity, which postulate some organic dysfunction in the brains or bodies of diagnosed persons, will of necessity bypass the possibility that what he takes as 'symptoms', to be related back to allegedly determinant antecedents, are aspects of those people's communicative relationships and have a sense apart from their being produced by physical organs—i.e. an interpersonal *meaning* or significance. Furthermore, the organic theorist will tend to ignore the interpersonal, purposive and cognitive aspects of the patient's activities and will focus more readily upon features such as catatonic stupor, affective disturbances or hallucinatory experiences—features that could more conceivably be the products of isolable biogenic variables. (Work on psychotomimetic drugs and sensory deprivation provides some rationale for this narrowing of the focus, although once the focus has been narrowed that way the results stand as only synecdochally related to some overall 'aetiology of schizophrenia'). Many cases diagnosed as 'paranoid' or 'paranoid schizophrenic' present, as their criterial attributes, coherent yet wild beliefs or systems of belief with few or no further evidences of bizarreness either physiologically or interpersonally. In these cases, biogenetic reserches have proven remarkably unfruitful, as the predominantly cultural violations of standards of appropriate or permissible belief characteristic of paranoid patients do not admit of biological reduction as easily as some other 'symptoms'. We have already alluded to the *ad hoc* basis of psychiatric diagnostics, and our remarks stand in the case of 'paranoia', but even if we accept that a homogeneous 'condition' of paranoia can be identified and look at some research predicated on that assumption, we find nothing to corroborate the biogenetic hypothesis. D. D. Jackson has remarked that in most measures reported in the literature, the paranoid patients show least deviation from stipulated physiological norms of weight and psychomotor efficiency and manifest a considerabel intactness of intelligence and the least dilapidation of habit patterns.[25] Shakow has noted that diagnosed paranoid patients resemble the 'normal' control personnel more often than they resemble other mental patients,[26] and Stevenson and his colleagues reported that their samples of diagnosed paranoids were unlike other categories in adrenocortical responses.[27] I shall return further on to discuss paranoia in a different context. At this point, I want to emphasise that it is precisely where *beliefs* are taken as 'symptoms' of some undiscovered biological abnormality that the solitary individual organism model peculiar to biogenetic work encounters most trouble.[28]

Biogenetic theorists of the aetiology of mental disorder cannot hope to achieve a statement of the necessary and sufficient conditions for

the holding of some bizarre belief or the communication of some
unusual experiences. There is a clear epistemological gap between
the language of cells, tissues and organs and the language of beliefs.
Neither do they attempt to locate some specific lesion and correlate
it with some specific delusion or pattern of conduct. Their aims are,
generally, to furnish explanations of patients' presentations which
demonstrate their reliance upon biochemically induced malfunctions
in the higher-order neurological substratum to ideation and action.
Put less rigorously, they seek to show that patients believe and act
the way they do because their thought processes are disordered by
virtue of some more or less specific structural imbalance in brain
biochemistry. Few organic aetiologists attempt a reduction of mental
concepts to physical ones in Carnapian fashion.[29]

The favoured approach of organic aetiologists has been the construction of 'model psychoses' by way of drug simulations or simple
theoretical election. Although clear descriptions of the phenomena
being researched at the 'molar' level are unavailable in such work,
we frequently find some outline of the model of the mental disorder
being employed, whilst the rest of the discussion is devoted to the
postulated organic correlates. Rado and his colleagues[30] developed
a simple clinical description of some typical characteristics of their
diagnosed schizophrenic sample. In their study, they emphasised the
apparent inability of their sample's constituent members to separate
out what to control group 'normals' were respectively painful and
pleasurable stimulations. On this basis, Heath[31] conceptualized the
'schizophrenic condition' as stemming from some imbalance in the
pain-pleasure continuum which he asserted might derive from a
disruption of limbic system activity by a faulty metabolism of amines.
Siegel, Niswander, Sachs and Stavros[32] were unable to confirm his
findings in their sample. Of course, the initial formulation by Rado
*et al* is open to the objection that the phenomena to which they
drew attention might be wholly irrelevant aetiologically both to their
sample's members and to any others with respect to those presentations that earned them their original diagnoses and hospitalisation.
Similar objections can be levelled against research designs which
extrapolate some particular presentation—e.g. the assertion by
patients of hallucinatory experiences—and erect programmes of
investigation into 'schizophrenia', as if that is all there is to it.

We inherit the disease model of insanity (or 'psychosis') in large
part from the pioneers of early German psychiatry. Alzheimer's

studies of the histopathology of the cerebral cortex influenced both Kraepelin and Bleuler,[33] and a biogenetic groundplan for psychiatric research was laid down to guide the production of a corpus of psychopathologic knowledge. Putting that plan into action involved treating the extant classificatory constructs as if they discriminated along *biologically relevant* dimensions. This assumption was to vitiate the programme as a whole in a number of ways, as we shall demonstrate. However, the medical model, although not replacing some monolithic 'demonological' one for mental disorders, did come into greater and greater prominence and psychiatry grew in prestige and, more importantly, in 'effectiveness' and humaneness of method. Psychopharmacology began, in the late pre-war and post-war periods, to make great strides; but S. Arieti's 1955 summary of the field of organic researches into *aetiology* concluded mournfully that 'no constructive avenue has yet been found in the organic field,'[34] and Kety's 1960 overview[35] told the same tale. Chemotherapeutic techniques, divorced from these aetiological endeavours, enabled psychiatrists to enter an era of constructive compassion on the basis of pragmatic experiment—only the monoamine oxidase inhibitors were the result of actual biochemical experimentation in laboratory conditions, but not of course on humans; they resulted from tests on the biochemical-neural correlates of lethargy in rats.

Much of the research conducted under the auspices of biochemists and clinical psychiatrists working jointly or in loose cooperation has been carried out with patients with a long history of hospitalisation and concomitant stigmatisation as insane, often institutionalised in conditions where overcrowding and mediocre standards of hygiene prevailed. Kety has commented that

> ... the development of a characteristic pattern of intestinal flora in a population of schizophrenic patients living together for long periods and fed from the same kitchen is a possibility which cannot be dismissed in interpreting what appear to be deviant metabolic pathways.[36]

An earlier review by R. K. McDonald[37] highlighted the fact that a dietary deficiency of vitamins had been found to explain at least two of the biochemical abnormalities attributed to the aetiology of schizophrenia. The action of phenothiazines and other chemotherapies, along with their metabolic products, effect changes occasionally attributed to 'the schizophrenic condition,' and residual biochemical transformations after repeated electroplexies might be added to this list of contaminations. Chlorpromazine, for example, (whose better-known tradename is Largactil) becomes metabolized to chlorpromazine sulphoxide which is chromatographically isomorphic with DMPE ('pink spot' extract), a substance thought at one time to be a peculiar product of schizophrenic patients and to be related to the aetiology of their condition. Recent research into a substance known as DMPEA (or 3, 4 Dimethoxyphenethylamine) has clearly questioned the implication of this substance in the aetiology of even a few cases of mental disorder. Shulgin, Sargent and Naranjo,[38] asking the question, 'is DMPEA a psychotomimetic agent?' (i.e. is it capable of inducing psychological changes as a result of effecting the neural system or CNS?) went ahead to administer controlled dosages to adult volunteers without any history of consultation with or hospitalisation by psychiatrists. They determined that, 'in no instance were any behavioural or psychotropic effects noted, nor were there any indications of autonomic disturbance,' and they concluded that 'the absence of any psychogenic properties speaks against its [DMPEA's] participation as a causal agent in the aetiology of the disease,'[39] Their maintenance of the disease terminology indicates perhaps that they are trying elsewhere within the framework of the same biochemical model of insanity, or at least that their faith in such a model has not been shaken by a negative empirical result.

One persistent and central theme in discussions of biochemical research in this area has been the issue of how to draw clear distinctions between factors thought to have aetiological power and factors arising out of the post-diagnostic experiences of the patients investigated. Put briefly, we are faced here with the issue of : cause *or* effect? One biochemist I know put this rather succinctly when he spoke of 'controlling for chronology'. Not surprisingly, no-one thinks that this problem can be settled in advance of considerations of concrete research findings. However, since all research into 'the schizophrenias' is of necessity *post hoc* (that is, after social and prefessional diagnostics have confirmed that identity on members of a sample), and since stress and anxiety induced by interpersonal reactions and hospitalisation itself can have biochemical correlates, this is in no sense a 'pseudo-problem'. It can only be seen as a non-problem against a background of thinking which conceives of the whole aetiological enterprise in psychopathology as a non-enterprise.

Alan A. Boulton's recent review of the scientific literature pertinent to our discussion[40] commences with a disarming prefatory remark :

'notwithstanding the controversies, progress has been slow if indeed there has been any,' and continues :

> To a biochemist it becomes apparent from the literature that schizophrenia is a difficult term; psychiatrists do not agree on a precise meaning and diagnosis for schizophrenia. A schizophrenic population certainly seems to be a mixed bag containing possibly several separate disease entities overlapping to some extent; their adequate separation and description are difficult because of inexact diagnostic criteria. This makes biochemical research much more difficult than in more definable conditions such as Parkinson's disease or certain inborn errors of metabolism[41].

Unfortunately, the despair over 'inexact diagnostic criteria' is likely to remain, since as we have noted, diagnoses in this field cannot be governed by fixed rules on the analogy with some physical conditions —interpersonal standards of conduct cannot be codified in the way in which we can codify physiological information. Nonetheless, what 'pathognomic aetiological agents' have in fact been posited? We have already schematically outlined a few of them. Amongst the remainder, we find work on the hypothesized hallucinogenic derivatives of epinephrine,[42] on the implication of ceruloplasmin and taraxein in cases of schizophrenia,[43] on bufotenin,[44] on thyroid function abnormalities,[45] on abnormality in cerebral oxygen circulation and consumption,[46] and on tryptophan metabolism. All have proven remarkably unproductive, even if we ignore for the moment their methodological adequacy. On the hypothesis that schizophrenic patients are such because of faulty endocrine functions, Manfred Bleuler, one of the world's leading clinicians, is quite dismissive; 'Clinical experience can easily be summarized in the statement : Endocrine patients are not schizophrenics and schizophrenics are not endocrine patients.'[47] Boulton concludes his survey of work on pathogenic metabolites with the statement : 'A critical survey of any single experiment in this field of toxic factors in schizophrenic blood [sic] leaves considerable doubts as to the significance of the findings and their relevance to schizophrenia.'[48]

There have been some frankly peculiar attempts to locate and isolate toxic substances in the bodies of labelled schizophrenic patients : extracts of urine from these patients have been injected into rats, spiders and Siamese fighting fish, the latter selected because of its known sensitivity to certain hallucinogens. No confirmation of reports that such injections induced electroencephalographic changes in these creatures was forthcoming and, contrary to earlier findings, an attempt to demonstrate lethargy in rats following the injection of cerebrospinal fluid from catatonic subjects was unsuccessful.[49] Differentiating between 'catatonics' and other classes of patient might be less susceptible to caprice than other forms of psychiatric diagnostic separations, but Boulton's review featured several allusions to 'chronic', 'acute' and 'simple' modalities of 'schizophrenia' without any clear indication of the actual presentations of patients so diagnosed. It is clear that some other researcher reading a paper which featured reference only to such a gross distinction as 'chronic' or 'simple' schizophrenia would not necessarily be in any position to match his own sample(s), and if he were to rely upon a psychiatrist to do that for him he would be forgetting the evidence on inter-psychiatric concordances and their rather sorry state (for his purposes, not for those of the practical psychiatric clinician). How does one rank a schizophrenic on a scale of greater or lesser chronicity? In terms of the greater or lesser unreasonableness of his beliefs, or the greater or lesser improprieties in his conduct, or the degree to which he holds to his beliefs or sustains his inappropriate lines of conduct? And if one elects a decision about that, one still has to operate on a clear notion of 'reasonabless' or 'propriety' that could withstand cross-contextual comparisons . . . . Devices such as the Minnesota Multiphasic Personality Inventory provide no real solution; not only do they rely upon some prior selection procedures to generate their testable subjects, but they simply impose a stock of redefinitions on those subjects which suffer from the same looseness and arbitrariness. Aetiologists work on the basis of a strict notion of scientific methodology in an area where such a notion is inapposite, and their attempts to force their subject matter into a tight, warrantable and determinate mould lead them to produce operationalizing devices that only serve to multiply their initial troubles. One wonders how many biochemical studies have not even been based upon such an attempt at controlling for replicability of findings—how many biochemically-researched samples included subjects manifesting such diverse 'symptoms' as unreasonable beliefs, grammatical distortion, hallucination, affective disturbance and withdrawal, respectively or conjointly, under the over-arching label of 'schizophrenia' in the name of generalizability, only for the researchers involved to be faced with another team's inability to replicate their findings.

Some researchers rely upon extended diagnostic scales such as 'schizophreniform disorders' to produce their samples, and do not appear in the least concerned about Maher's point that there may be 'many behavioural phenomena of differing aetiologies which are all classed together as schizophrenic [and this] must be borne in mind whenever we are attempting to discover some order in the [scientific] materials'[50]—a clear reference to the 'mixed-bag' issue mentioned in Boulton's review cited earlier. Occasionally, the problem will be mentioned, but its practical research implications glossed over and ignored. David Rosenthal, for instance, whose collaborative work on the genetic transmission of schizophrenia is predicated upon the use of the vague label of 'schizophreniform disorder', can write : 'It is this heterogeneity of manifestation in all phases and aspects of the illness that makes the evaluation of aetiological factors such a precarious enterprise,' and yet assert that his findings importantly substantiate the genetic transmission hypothesis.[51]

On the basis of a twenty-three year longitudinal study of 208 people diagnosed as schizophrenic, Manfred Bleuler noted that there is some difficulty in reconciling somatic theories of schizophrenia as a disease with the facts about the frequency and scope of transformations that take place in their conduct. Often, these transformations are sufficient for discharge to be allowed, and those discharged live in the community quite routinely once again some years after the 'onset' of those performances which elicited the original diagnosis of 'schizophrenia'.[52] Harry Stack Sullivan also made reference to changes in catatonic patients which were sometimes quite radical,[53] and Norman Cameron remarked on the reversibility of previously fixed communicative styles that characterized patients in his samples.[54] These observations tend to reinforce the view that, amongst those populations characterized as schizophrenic, there may well be people whose situations cannot adequately be understood in terms of metabolic errors, brain atrophy and so on. Moreover, the work of Chapman[55] and the survey by Williams[56] are both instructive on the question of the distinct limits that exist for comparison between brain-syndrome speech and conduct and the various sorts of speech and conduct characteristic of at least a number of diagnosed psychotics. The whole question of thought disorder will be raised again in a later chapter.

Throughout this discussion, I have been bracketing the issue of the relationship between biochemical and genetic researches in psychopathology. In fact, little of the work done by biochemists so far has any bearing on the sort of work done by hereditarian theorists, with the possible exception of research into metabolic error. Even here, however, it could hardly be claimed that the mediations between genotype and phenotype (inheritance and conduct) were being traced in a careful manner with samples stratified according to the relevances of *both* the biochemist and the geneticist. There has been a rather surprising absence of dialogue (at least, in publication) between the hereditarians or behavioural geneticists and their colleagues in the wider somatic field, with the result that genetic transmissions are claimed with no specification of the biochemical agency or mediating process involved—there are broad statements about heredity on the basis of statistical inference but rarely a mention of the sort of biochemical research that might presumably corroborate these at the organic level itself. The actual evidence on the genetic transmission hypothesis is open to no clear cut interpretation, as Weil-Malherbe[57] and Rosenbaum[58] have indicated. Kaplan[59] and Baldessarini[60] have shown the limitations of the single locus autosomal genetic model of the type used by Kallman in his early studies,[61] and D. D. Jackson has sharply drawn attention to the problems of a genuinely Mendelian programme of research : we humans have no pure stocks to begin with, we do not breed together brother and sister and, especially, human environments cannot remain constant as required formally in Mendelian studies.[62] Bleuler has pointed out that :

> The view that schizophrenia is transmitted from one generation to the next through a pathogenic gene, according to Mendel's law, has become quite improbable. Family histories and the number of schizophrenics among relatives of schizophrenics do not support such an assumption. A further important argument against the Mendelian theory of schizophrenia is found in the fact that schizophrenics are much less fertile in comparison to the general population .... We can exclude the possibility that the essential background of schizophrenia consists in one or a few pathogenic genes which influence the brain by an error of metabolism.[63]

The standardisation of research populations in the genetic field is as poor as in the other main areas of somatic research, based as they all are upon the evaluations and context bound pragmatic judgements of clinicians or psychiatrically trained researchers themselves. As this is the case, we cannot derive any solace from counting up relatives and finding out how many have been diagnosed as 'schizophrenic' and relating such a count to the current predicament of the present sample. Moreover, a decision about a person's psychiatric status is not necessarily finalized at the point of hospitalization—sometimes, a retrospective reconstitution of the former view of his condition will be made. L. Penrose[64] found, in an early study, that in England 33% of first admissions were diagnosed 'schizophrenic' and 17% as 'manic-depressive', whilst after twenty years the diagnosis of schizophrenia in these cases had risen to 69.8% and the diagnosis of manic-depression had fallen to 7.4%. The chances that one would have been diagnosed as schizophrenic can be said to have increased with each year spent inside a mental hospital. Bernard Rimland, in a review of the biogenetic evidence that is largely favourable to an organic hypothesis,[65] noted that the literature in psychiatry is replete with : 'cases of patients called psychogenetic and given psychotherapy only to succumb to an undetected brain tumour or degenerative CNS disease,'[66] and work by Ross[67] and Malamud[68] is cited in corroboration. Rimland suggests that as present neurological and EEG methods often fail to reveal even *gross* brain pathology which is clearly visible upon post-mortem examinations,'[69] we should be careful about attributing social or psychological causation to individual mental patients; but this sceptical note might be turned the other way around—for if that is the case, then undetected and determinant contaminations may well affect the members of samples taken to be suffering from 'schizophrenia' due to postulated biochemical or genetically-based malfunctions. Reclassification can take place *posthumously*. So what *is* it that is supposed to be genetically transmitted?

Jan Böök[70] has remarked that all genetic diseases are basically metabolic defects. The problem, then, for him, is that : 'the pathway from these original intracellular metabolic defects to the symptoms and signs that can be observed by the clinician, and sometimes only with elaborate scientific techniques, is generally enormous.' Apart from the mediation problem he raises, Böök refers to the observation of 'the symptoms and signs' that sometimes can only be observed with 'elaborate scientific techniques'. Yet the symptoms and signs of insanity can be observed by any culturally competent person, and a psychiatrist uses the available standards of cultural comportment and the rest as arbiters in making his diagnosis. Clinicians do not require special techniques—only their judgemental equipment. Perhaps here Böök is making reference to the battery of operational devices such as the MMPI already mentioned. If so, their status as either 'elaborate' or 'scientific' is questionable. One wonders what *clinicians* could possibly be looking for which necessitates the adoption of techniques other than those furnished by their own faculties. The real mediation problem is surely concerned with tracing the actual biochemical realisations of the inherited defects, and that is not the task of a clinician. It is certainly a lot to ask of a clinician that he (a) decide *finally* about a case solely for research purposes, (b) decide *fairly* about a case when there are several imponderables over which he can exert no control, such as disguised CNS disease or other covert physical pathology and (c) decide in concordance with some nonexistent *norm* of diagnostic ranking; all in the aid of a basically spurious nomothetic enterprise.

Data for many genetic studies in psychopathology derive from hospital charts, local authority records and word of mouth reports on dead relatives. The first two are not compiled for purposes of explicit research, but for some range of practical purposes, whilst the latter can, of course, hardly ever be conclusive with respect to accuracy. Thus, the correspondence between what such representations are claimed to represent and their manifest content is decided unilaterally and 'by fiat'.[71] In other words, they are supposed to picture or mirror literally some set of facts about the background of psychiatric patients, whereas they record some set of facts in the terms and relevance system appropriate for some everyday contingencies. Often, researchers use coded materials produced organisationally as if those professional, practical purposes that informed their production dovetailed with the requirements of scientific work. Epidemiological work (whose utility is discussed below) provides some of the resources for work based on a knowledge of gene pool composition. More rigorous research has employed Galton's method of examining monozygotic (identical) twins to detect concordances for 'schizophrenia' which could then be claimed as attributable to the same genetic predetermination. The most celebrated example of this sort of approach is that of Kallman.[72] Kallman found that in 86% of the cases in his sample where one identical twin had been diagnosed 'schizophrenic' the other twin was also diagnosed as such. The concordance rate for fraternal twins was 14%. Kallman believed that he had thereby demonstrated a genotypic substratum to 'the schizophrenic disease'.

Don D. Jackson's brilliant critique of Kallman's work[73] pinpointed three central issues. Firstly, Kallman dichotomized his twins sample under two headings : 'separated' and 'non-separated'. The former referred to separation from one another *only five years' prior* to the psychiatric diagnosis—most of the twins remained together until well past the usual age for marriage. Secondly, only two cases of mono-zygotic twins reared apart and processed through psychiatric agencies as schizophrenic occurred in the literature of the forty years prior to 1960 and, considering the high rate for the diagnosis, these cases could be accounted for simply on a chance basis. Thirdly, not only was the environment left to vary randomly, but negative family histories were glossed over. There is more to Jackson's case than this, and the reader is urged to consult it for himself (although to be wary of Jackson's psychodynamics approach to the problem, which is more than somewhat metaphysical). Suffice to remark here, then, that Kallman's concordances are open to a range of competing *ad hoc* explanations. Neither Kallman nor any other hereditarians of his day made any allowance in their claims for the possibility that clinicians, perhaps acting in concert with family doctors, might have been pre-disposed to make the same diagnosis for a monozygotic twin present-ing quite different interpersonal 'clinical' characteristics from his brother or sister if those clinicians harboured a hereditarian pre-judice. Moreover, Kallman—again, amongst others—largely ignored the issue of 'symptom concordance' and whether or not the proband twin sets manifested a transient or more lasting mode of problematic self-presentation. If transient cases were listed alongside more lasting cases, then we might be reading of a 'disease concordance rate' which could be considerably reduced if we removed the tran-sients. This point stems from Essen-Moller's discussion.[74]

The work of Pollin, Stabenau and Tupin,[75] which favours an intrafamilial sociological model of the 'aetiology of schizophenia,' records twenty six cases of *discordance* in the development of psychiatric problems in twins, and Tienari,[76] Gottesman,[77] and Kringlen[78] all give evidence to show that discordant monozygotic twins turn up as often or more frequently than concordant pairs. Of course, given the possibility that CNS dysfunctions might be turning up in samples labelled 'schizophrenic', it is not unlikely that some concordances might be attributable to clear organic problems, although since we lack phenotypical criteria for making such dis-criminations on the basis of people's conduct, there is no satisfactory method for resolving this 'contamination'.

There is one intriguing way of glossing the discordance problem.

This involves postulating 'latency' or non-actualised 'predisposition'; it does not matter whether any particular individual does or does not 'develop' modes of conduct that elicit a clinician's diagnosis of schizophrenia; what is important, runs the argument, is that if 'X' has the implicated 'hereditary factors' then he is *basically* or *potentially* schizophrenic. Those who take this line argue that the discordant monozygotic twin of a diagnosed schizophrenic 'has a *forme fruste* of the disease, whether we can detect it clinically or not'.[79] This approach has but one dubious advantage; the guarantee of irrefutability to its proponents—who thereby explain nothing. It is a matter for imaginative conjecture as to what appearances might conceivably constitute 'basic', 'latent' or 'potential' schizophrenia. Since insanity of any sort can only be constituted as such, can only be seen, through the operation of culturally available recognition practices, talk of latent and potential schizophrenia is without coherence. One might add that in speaking at all of schizophrenia as a disease, latent or otherwise, even the psychiatric subtypes tend to be forgotten; it is extremely rare to find an investigation being conducted or reported on the biochemical or genetic origins of '*paranoid* schizophrenia', for example.

The era in which behavioural geneticists aimed at nothing less than a complete explanation of the incidence of 'schizophrenia' is now, I think, behind us. The contemporary disputes are waged in terms of the levels of genetic *contribution* to the condition. That is, there is some agreement that schizophrenia, in any of its subtypes, is the product of interaction between a genetically 'predisposed' subject and his sociophysical environment. This assumption has had the effect of enabling theorists to account for variances by citing the possibility that, wherever a discordance arises, some failure of the sociophysical environment to 'actualize' the condition can be posited. (Of course, this sort of theoretical stop-gapping works the other way around as well—sociogenic aetiologists, finding variances or cases that do not fit in with their models, can cite absence of genetic predisposition). But it has yet to be demonstrated that any genetically inherited disorder, whether it be endocrinological or some genetic morphism, can be suppressed or brought out by specific sorts of social experiences. Penrose concluded a famous paper by remarking that the variability of 'clinical types', onset periods, age and incidence rules out most genetic accounts *a priori*,[80] and the genetically-informed psychopathologist who favours an interactional account of the causation of schizophrenic conditions has yet to use any such account in concrete terms to deal with such variability in a rigorous manner.

I think that an important problem which few hereditarians really face is the problem of *symptomatological discontinuities* that occur in patients who are diagnosed as schizophrenic. By this, I mean to refer to the many case histories that are available which show that a number of patients display intermittently, rather than continuously, the sort of conduct and/or belief(s) which elicited community labelling and psychiatric ratification as insane. Manfred Bleuler has noted that, for his long-term sample of diagnosed schizophrenic patients, the 'healthy life'

> ... is never simplified and finally extinguished as in progressive organic psychoses .... (e.g. neurosyphilitic conditions) The schizophrenic psychosis can neither be characterised by the final loss of any function nor by the production of any new morbid process.[81]

Bleuler is one clinician amongst many, and it is as well to bear in mind our arguments about clinical agreements, but his observations must qualify any rash general statements that seek to portray *the* schizophrenic condition as in every important respect paralleling those conditions with known and determinate organic substrata. Only longitudinal clinical studies like Bleuler's can effectively dispel the myth that all persons labelled schizophrenic undergo progressive degeneration of essentially the same functions.

There are several sorts of considerations which lead people to the view that patients diagnosed as schizophrenic exhibit generalized personal dilapidation and continuous incomprehensibility. One source of the idea is probably the media—press and television—although more recently there has been some evidence that more subtle clinical assessments are being aired in the popular press and on television programmes concerned especially with documenting the nature of insanity. However, since it is mainly orthodox psychopathologists who present the theoretical aspects of insanity to the public there is still a tendency for overgeneralized assertion and the disease model of schizophrenia to prevail. That, of course, is an expression of my point of view. But I have found that both lay observers and professionals from outside mental hospitals who are doing work in and for psychiatry treat their experiences of inmate mental patients in a way that is all too readily influenced by mental hospital orderings of patient activity. That is, for students, social workers and some others who have occasion to make visits to mental institutions, the impression gained is often that inmates are basically as helpless as their demeanour suggests; that they are without active initiative and perceive themselves as ill and that they require the constant supervision which they have solely on account of the nature of their common condition. I think that some of the work on the degree to which patients suffer from 'institutionalization' and related studies that tend to show that at least some are able to carry on routine community life whilst harbouring their odd beliefs, etc, in private, have contributed to our understanding of the extent to which the sorts of administrative constraints and pragmatic psychiatric custodial policies structure the options for rational action in mental hospitals. The regimen and social organisation of mental hospitals can be a serious delimiter of options for self-assertion in rationally appearing ways on the part of many patients, and both Goffman[82] and Kahne[83] have written sensitively about the everyday constraints on patients and the ways in which adaptation to the social organisation of mental hospitals of certain types can only lead logically to the abrogation of just those styles of behaviour which might enhance patients' chances of seeming rational. Further, since the rhetoric of psychopathology rationalizes acts of frustration or rebellion against the total institutional matrix of hospitals and clinics in terms of the categories of the disease model—i.e. as further symptoms of sickness—then it becomes more clear how careful one has to be to disentangle the facts about a patient's 'condition' from the facts about how he adapts to and is perceived within an institution.

I am not engaged here in criticizing mental hospitals in general or any mental hospital in particular. What I am doing is trying to indicate some of the reasons why people may find my arguments about the heterogeneity of schizophrenic conduct and population characteristics somewhat exaggerated. Clinicians of some experience probably will not, but I cannot be sure. All I can do here is to rely on both the available documentation of a plethora of cases and the argument from institutionalization. Since the disease theory of schizophrenia draws for some of its clinical support on evidence from clinicians who use the same theory as a resource for interpreting and dealing with their subjects, I think that it is only reasonable to point out that a wider-based perspective might set things in sharper focus.

When I spoke of 'disentangling' the facts about a patient's 'condition' from the facts about how he is adapted to and perceived within his hospital setting I was not suggesting that there is a pristine 'individual condition' and then, superimposed onto that, his ways of acting within a social setting. It is clear that a person's ways of acting within social settings are the grounds on which *any* judgement about his psychological status must be based. Rather, I was alluding to the proposition that a person's spontaneous social orientations, however insane they may be, can be made to seem stereotyped and congruent with an image of a diseased organism under conditions of obedience to or hostility against certain sorts of organizational constraints. I think that John H. Weakland was entertaining considerations of this kind when he wrote :

> Quite simply, the nature of studies of schizophrenia, like their object, is very much enmeshed in and influenced by practical rather than scientific considerations. People acting in crazy ways, and methods of labelling and dealing with them (that is, conceptions of mental disease, diagnosis, hospitals and record-keeping, and so on) are urgent practical matters of social life, for individuals and for the social system. Correspondingly, these are deeply entwined with systems that are highly ordered ..., that is, with the administrative, legal, and medical systems in our society, or their analogues in customary behaviour elsewhere. Such systems, quite expectably, are normative; they are geared and ordered toward handling certain selected problems within established social frameworks and limits, not toward the clarification and understanding of basic general relationships among social phenomena. There is a natural tendency in research work toward utilizing the ordering represented in these established categories and procedures ...[84]

I shall return to the issue of cultural underpinnings to psychopathology, its theories and practice, in later discussion. At this point, I want to look at the last of the biogenetic studies of insanity with which I am going to deal in this chapter—the adoptive twin studies. I treat this somewhat separately because it is a new development and is heralded as marking a breakthrough in hereditarian research methodology. The adoptive studies involve analyses of the types and prevalence of diagnosed schizophrenia in the biological and adoptive families of schizophrenic cases who have been adopted.[85]

The researches of Kety, Rosenthal, Wender and Schulsinger[86] were carried out using the notion of 'schizophrenia spectrum disorders' as the operative 'type' being investigated. In a recent paper outlining a further programme of hereditarian research the same notion is used by Rosenthal[87] to include 'doubtful', 'borderline' ('psycho-neurotic') schizophrenics, reactive, process and chronic schizophrenics, schizo-affective types, schizoids and paranoids. Although Rosenthal is frank about the exacerbation of the diagnostic reliability question in using such 'fringe' classifications, he seems to see no fundamental problem in conducting research into 'schizophrenia' with such a wide range of types subsumed under that rubric. He considers that if he were to restrict himself to 'hard core' cases, his sample would be too small to warrant the sort of inferences he seeks to make. But it is hard to imagine what sort of inferences he *could* warrant on the basis of research into such a motley collection.

Leon Eisenberg noted his discomfort with such a widely extensive scale of 'disorder types' when it was mooted as part of the original work on adoptive index cases :

> ... once one includes psychopathology in a continuum from process to reactive schizophrenia to personality disorder, alcoholism, eccentricity and even talent (as Dr Karlsson is willing to do), one faces a formidable problem in differentiating environ-mental phenocopies which surely must occur the more frequently the further out on the spectrum we search.[88]

Karlsson's idea of the 'superphrenic' is one of accounting for discordant MZ twins, but quite how he can seriously incorporate such a unilateral moral devaluation of the talents of the identical twin of a schizophrenic case in order to render unequivocal his genetic theory is something that only he could account for. It does seem to me, however, that any statistical superstructure erected on research conducted into such a morass of disparate phenomena would constitute a scientific mirage.

In their adoptive studies, the researchers were trying to 'control for' social environmental 'effects'. They relied upon abstracted case histories, but noted the possibility that knowledge of the relation-ship existing between an index case and a member of his biological family : 'could have affected the tendency to notice, to record, to institutionalize, or to diagnose schizophrenia spectrum disorder in one or the other individual on the part of professional or nonprofes-sional observers, especially if there was a prevalent belief that schizo-phrenia was inherited'.[89] I have already touched on this possibility in my discussion of Kallman's work. In the absence of any knowledge of base rates for psychiatric diagnoses for various areas, we cannot tell to what extent a clinician would tend to diagnose a twin or sibling of a known hospitalized subject as a member of the same diagnostic class, but I know that some approved GPs and psychiatric professionals invoke the same labels without hesitation on the basis of a strong genetic bias.

Foster studies of twins or other relatives cannot of themselves provide genetic evidence of anything. They may be used to give impressionistic guides as to the effect or lack of effect of specific environments. However, T. Lidz, a proponent of a family interaction model of schizophrenia, was quite able to criticise the adoptive studies on the grounds that since the interaction processes of the adoptive families were not studied, these remained 'uncontrolled variables' in the research design and results.[90]

I do not want to end on a purely negative note, even though I have been trying to show that the piecemeal psychopathologic studies of schizophrenia in biochemistry and behaviour genetics do not fit into the explanatory mosaic we are promised as a logical culmination of research efforts. I want to state what genuinely useful scientific findings *can* be expected from aetiologists of an organic persuasion.

The scientific enterprise in which somaticists and hereditarians are engaged should properly be conceived as one of seeking out and dealing with some category or categories of disease hitherto undiscovered which can be found in some persons diagnosed on the basis of quite varied contingencies as 'schizophrenic' in one mode or another; but the sublanguage in which psychopathology expresses its organic research, developed in collusion with the practical interests of psychiatry, frames that enterprise misleadingly in terms of research into 'the aetiology of schizophrenia,' '...of psychosis,' '...of insanity,' etc. Moreover, since we shall never be in a position logically to state the necessary and sufficient antecedent conditions for any person to become diagnosed as 'schizophrenic' (the social contingencies ramify over and above any biological ones), talk of work on the 'causation' of the schizophrenias is idle. Currently, aetiologists appear to hope that a few replications will furnish them grounds for claiming that a real relationship between their postulated variables has been demonstrated; but not only does the evidence on diagnostic variation and its evaluative basis cast doubt upon the level of generality that any such work could attain, there is also the vexed question of what a 'control group' could look like which would in any sense be relevant to the phenomena under consideration. What features could a control group be selected to control for? The heterogeneity of control group personnel matches the heterogeneity of processed schizophrenics, so the matching of normals to schizophrenics is largely an ad hoc procedure that needs to be carried out afresh on each occasion of research experimentation. Standardisation over cases is rarely discussed as an attainable goal in the biogenetics literature.

If we can hope only for information on new brain and CNS diseases from work purportedly carried out into the 'causes of schizophrenia' (and the word 'only' is not intended to be in the least disparaging), then it seems rather superfluous to attempt to enshrine the contemporary psychiatric taxonomy in the way in which some researchers feel they must. Such a taxonomy is a starting-point for work on the biological foundations of specific disorders in cognitive functioning—but it is too often treated as having genuine discriminatory value for organic research. What is required, I believe, is recognition of the view that within the scope of populations of diagnosed schizophrenics there may be people suffering from the same kind of lesion, and that these people may well have nothing biologically in common with others of their diagnostic group in terms of their actual presentations. The diagnostic categories arise from our social and moral needs, and there is no reason to think that they also describe exactly correlated physical dysfunctions. What is called schizophrenic is so variable that it is hopeless to expect that something so variable will relate strictly to physical constants. As A. R. Louch has put it,

> It would be unreasonable to expect chemical categories of mental disorder to preserve the kinds of distinction currently enshrined under such labels as paranoid or schizophrenic, hysteric or compulsive .... Even if there were a rough identity of reference, we should be misled in speaking of blood chemistry as the cause of (social) errors, for it would be irrelevant to appeal to causes as grounds for correctness .... If we look at this behaviour from a physiological or medical point of view, we must discard the psychiatrist's terms along with the method of appraisal ...[91]

The success of biochemical methods of treatment of patients diagnosed as schizophrenic in any of its subtypes has reinforced the blanket view that organic research into the schizophrenias is likely to provide an explanatory framework which links descriptions of phenomenal presentations to quantified descriptions of causally efficient physiological states. I want briefly to dispel the assumptions underlying this position. Primarily, the strong version of this perspective argues from success in treatment to similarity in status of treatment medium and causative agent. Bernard Rimland, for example, suggests that successes with certain psychotropic drugs 'provide a strong impetus' towards a biogenetic conclusion.[92] He goes on to note that the experimental inculcation of 'psychotic-like behaviour' in volunteer subjects by biochemical inputs adds 'weight to the biogenic position'. Yet he was quite prepared to knock down this sort of argument when it was deployed by behaviourist students of the neuroses—he suggested there that he could not concur in the idea that 'because in laboratory-type studies you may be able to manipulate a normal person into temporarily acquiring a very specific behaviour of a bizarre sort, *all* bizarre behaviour must have been similarly produced'.[93] Since the intake of amphetamine at certain levels induces conduct like that of forms of paranoia, then it might, on Rimland's logic, be proposed that all forms of paranoia stem from the intake or self-manufacture of amphetamines; it is obvious that the relationship between the two is wholly contingent. There is, of course, no reason to suppose that because tranquilisers can ease my depression then my depression was the product of those physical processes which tranquilisers tranquilise, since I might have any number of reasons for being depressed. There are no logical grounds for arguing here from the status of the treatment medium to the status of the precipitating medium.

Throughout this chapter, I have had to use the terminology of my adversaries in order to argue effectively with them on their own terrain. But in doing so, I may have given the impression that I think insanity is the kind of phenomenon (or phenomena) for which causal accounts might properly be given. 'Aetiology' is, after all, a word that means 'causation' in its medical use. The most that we can logically aspire to are accounts of cases that yield data on dysfunctions in the organic substrata to higher-order mental functioning. This does *not* mean that we shall ever be in a position to specify the exact relationship between events in the brain and nervous system and the observed speech and conduct of individuals, and certainly not in any causal sense. What it does indicate is the proper metatheoretical claim for somatic research : 'X, Y and Z have been discovered to exist and to affect the brain functions of certain people diagnosed as schizophrenic—this will enable us to reclassify those particular people as physically ill.'

In delineating some of the constraints, logical and substantive, which operate in this field, and in criticizing certain researches, programmes and claims, I did not intend to minimize the importance of organic research into what goes on inside mental patients; what I wanted to assert was that the discovery of any new brain or CNS disease or malfunction might be held back by the enshrinement of psychiatric taxonomy as the sample-generating basis in such research. But even then, somaticists cannot have the last word on insanity.

## NOTES

1. The term 'paradigm' is taken from Thomas S. Kuhn. In his work, *The Structure of Scientific Revolutions* University of Chicago Press, (1962), Kuhn uses the term to refer to, amongst other things, a constellation of scientific puzzles, a common theme in a cluster of research programmes, a scientific tradition, a classic work, a standard illustration, a way of looking at things and, the use we borrow, an epistemological viewpoint unifying the whole or a large part of a scientific discipline. Margaret Masterman has found that Kuhn, in the work cited, uses the word 'in not less than twenty-one different senses'. (M. Masterman 'The Nature of a Paradigm' in I. Lakatos & A. Musgrave (eds.) *Criticism and the Growth of Knowledge* Cambridge University Press (1970) pp. 59-89)

2. David Mechanic *Medical Sociology* New York, (1968) p. 15

3. D. P. Ausubel 'Personality Disorder *Is* Disease' in Thomas J. Scheff (ed.) *Mental Illness and Social Processes* Harper & Row (1967) p. 259

4. W. A. Scott 'Research Definitions of Mental Health and Mental Illness' *Psychological Bulletin* vol. 55 (January 1958) pp. 29-45

5. For some documentation of this, see Anselm Strauss, Leonard Schatzman, Rue Bucher *et al Psychiatric Ideologies and Institutions* Glencoe, Free Press (1964) passim

6. The conception of 'tacit knowledge' is taken from M. Polanyi *Personal Knowledge: Towards a Post-Critical Philosophy* University of Chicago Press (1958). Harold Garfinkel has also discussed the problem of correspondence between research descriptions in the non-biological human sciences and the phenomena being described in the following: 'In reading a journal account for the purpose of literal replication, researchers who attempt to reconstruct the relationship between the reported procedures and the results frequently encounter a gap of insufficient information. The gap occurs when the reader asks how the investigator decided the correspondence between what was actually observed and the intended event for which the actual observation is treated as its evidence. The reader's problem consists in having to decide that the reported observation is a literal instance of the intended occurrence, i.e. that the actual observation

and the intended occurrence are identical *in sense*. Since the relationship between the two is a sign relationship, the reader must consult some set of grammatical rules to decide this correspondence. This grammar consists in some theory of the intended events on the basis of which the decisions to code the actual observations as findings are recommended. It is at this point that the reader must engage in interpretive work and an assumption of 'underlying' matters 'just known in common' about the society in terms of which, what the respondent said, is treated as synonymous with what the observer meant.' (*Studies in Ethnomethodology*, Prentice-Hall (1967), pp. 95-6)

　7.　D. Bannister 'The Logical Requirements for Research into Schizophrenia' *British Journal of Psychiatry* vol. 114 (1968) pp. 181-88

　8.　See Abraham Kaplan *The Conduct of Inquiry* San Francisco, Chandler Press (1964)

　9.　Brendan A. Maher *Introduction to Research in Psychopathology* McGraw-Hill (1970) p. 37. The discussion of construct validity draws on Bernard S. Phillips, *Social Research* New York, Macmillan (1966)

　10　Barbara Wootton *Social Science and Social Pathology* Allen & Unwin (1959) p. 225 et seq

　11.　R. D. Laing *The Politics of Experience and The Bird of Paradise* Penguin (1968)

　12.　Thomas S. Szasz 'The Psychiatric Classification of Behaviour: A Strategy of Personal Constraint' in Leonard D. Eron (ed.) *The Classification of Behaviour Disorders* Aldine Publishing Co. (1966) pp. 123-70

　13.　R. Arnoff 'Some Factors Influencing the Unreliability of Clinical Judgements' *Journal of Clinical Psychology* vol. 10 (1954). P. Ash in his paper 'The Reliability of Psychiatric Diagnosis' *Journal of Abnormal and Social Psychology* vol. 44 (1949) pp. 272-77 found that substantial variations in diagnoses extended even to the most experienced clinicians.

　14.　Aron Beck 'Reliability of Psychiatric Diagnosis: A Critique of Systematic Studies' *American Journal of Psychiatry* vol. 119 (1962) pp. 210-16

　15.　J. Zubin 'Classification of the Behavioural Disorders' in P. Farnsworth (ed.) *Annual Review of Psychology* vol. 18 (1967)

　16.　N. Kreitman, P. Sainsbury, J. Morrissey, J. Towers & J. Scrivener 'The Reliability of Psychiatric Diagnosis: An Analysis' *Journal of Mental Science* vol. 107 (1961) pp. 887-908

　17.　E. Zigler & L. Phillips 'Psychiatric Diagnosis and Symptomatology' *Journal of Abnormal and Social Psychology* vol. 63 (1961)

　18.　R. Freudenberg & J. Robertson 'Symptoms in Relation to Psychiatric Diagnosis and Treatment' *Archives of Neurology and Psychiatry* vol. 76 (1956)

　19.　M. G. Sandifer Jnr., C. Pettus & D. Quade 'A Study of Psychiatric Diagnosis' *Journal of Nervous and Mental Diseases* vol. 139 (1964)

　20.　J. Katz *et al.* 'Studies of the Diagnostic Process' *American Journal of Psychiatry* vol. 125 (1969)

　21.　Harold Garfinkel 'The Rational Properties of Scientific and Commonsense Activities' in his *Studies in Ethnomethodology* Prentice-Hall

(1967) pp. 262-83

22.   Thomas S. Szasz 'The Myth of Mental Illness' *The American Psychologist* vol. 15 (February 1960) pp. 113-118 and his recent book *Ideology and Insanity: Essays on the Psychiatric Dehumanisation of Man* Doubleday-Anchor (1970)

23   David Cooper *Psychiatry and Anti-Psychiatry* Tavistock Publications (1967)

24.   K. Kolle *An Introduction to Psychiatry* New York, Philosophical Library (1963) p. 7

25.   Don D. Jackson 'Introduction' to his edited collection of research into *The Aetiology of Schizophrenia* Basic Books (1960)

26.   D. Shakow 'Segmental Set' *Archives of General Psychiatry* vol. 6 (1962) pp. 1-17

27.   J. A. F. Stevenson, J. B. Derrick, G. E. Hobbs, & E. V. Metcalfe 'Adrenocortical Response and Phosphate Excretion in Schizophrenia' *Archives of Neurology and Psychiatry* vol. 78 (1957) pp. 312-20

28.   J. S. Tyhurst 'Paranoid Patterns' in A. H. Leighton, J. A. Clausen & R. Wilson (eds.) *Exploration in Social Psychiatry* Basic Books (1957) Chapter Two

29.   For Carnap, 'a sentence about other minds refers to physical processes in the body of the person in question. On any other interpretation the sentence becomes untestable in principle, and thus meaningless' (R. Carnap 'Psychology in Physical Language' *Erkenntnis* 111 (1932-33)) This stems from his assertion that a sentence says no more than what is testable about it. Carnap has, of course, been widely criticized for confusing statements of fact with sentences in general, and in this verificationist philosophical psychology he provides no means for dealing with first-person active psychological statements where the notion of verification is inapposite. Norman Malcolm, in his 'Behaviourism as a Philosophy of Psychology' in T. W. Wann (ed.) *Behaviourism and Phenomenology: Contrasting Bases for Modern Psychology,* University of Chicago Press (1964) pp. 141-55, has argued against the Skinnerian variant of Carnap's reductionism, in which Skinner suggested that first person psychological utterances are reports of private stimuli; such utterances as 'I've a bad headache' are not based upon observations of flushed face, dull eyes or intracerebral pressures. In fact, it makes little sense to say that such utterances are constative reports in the first place. Rather, following Austin, they are *performatives,* expressing pain in the same sort of way as crying or grimacing expresses pain. Moreover, it would be odd to say that someone could misreport his own pain, could be mistaken in his observations of his inner processes, and where one cannot speak of correctness and incorrectness of observation intelligibly, it seems logical to suppose that even to speak of 'observation' is misplaced. Of course, few mental patients make performative utterances that get mistranslated as reports on their own pathology in organic researches!

30.   S. Rado *et al* 'Schizotypal Organisation: A Preliminary Report on a Clinical Study of Schizophrenia' in S. Rado & G. Daniels (eds.) *Changing Concepts of Psychoanalytic Medicine* New York, Grune and

Stratton (1956)

31.  R. G. Heath 'A Biochemical Hypothesis on the Etiology of Schizophrenia' in D. D. Jackson (ed.) *The Aetiology of Schizophrenia* New York, Basic Books (1960)

32.  M. Siegel *et al* 'Taraxein: Fact or Artifact?' *American Journal of Psychiatry* vol. 115 (1959) pp. 819-20

33.  See Seymour S. Kety 'Recent Biochemical Theories of Schizophrenia' in D. D. Jackson (ed.) op. cit. p. 121

34.  Silvano Arieti *Interpretation of Schizophrenia* Robert Brunner (1955) p. 9

35.  S. S. Kety 'Recent Biochemical Theories . . .' op. cit.

36.  ibid p. 122

37.  R. K. McDonald 'Problems in Biologic Research in Schizophrenia' *Journal of Chronic Disorders* vol. 8 (1958)

38.  A. T. Shulgin, T. Sargent & C. Naranjo 'The Role of 3, 4 Dimethoxyphenephthylamine in Schizophrenia' *Nature,* vol. 212 (December 1966), pp. 1606-7

39.  ibid p. 1607

40.  A. A. Boulton 'Biochemical Research in Schizophrenia' *Nature,* vol. 231, May 1971, pp. 22-28

41.  ibid p. 22

42.  This thesis was first advanced by H. Osmond & J. Smithies in 'Schizophrenia: A New Approach' *Journal of Mental Science* vol. 98 (1952) pp. 309-15. There were several attempts to test the theory. S. Szara, J. Axelrod & S. Perlin, in their paper 'Is Adrenochrome Present in the Blood?' noted that, using techniques of high sensitivity, they were still unable to detect adrenochrome in the blood of control 'normals' and in the blood of diagnosed 'acute' and 'chronic' schizophrenics, and R. Holland, G. Cohen, M. Goldenberg, J. Sha & A. I. Leifer, in their paper 'Adrenaline and Noradrenaline in the Urine and Plasma of Schizophrenics' *Fed. Proc.* vol. 17 (1958) p. 378, found no differences in the manner in which circulating adrenaline was utilised and destroyed in 'normals' and diagnosed schizophrenic patients. (Epinephrine is U.S. jargon for adrenaline).

43.  See M. Siegel *et al,* op. cit., and R. K. McDonald's paper, 'Plasma Ceruloplasmin and Ascorbic Acid Levels in Schizophrenia' (Presented to the 1957 Annual Meeting of the American Psychiatric Association in Chicago and cited in S. S. Kety, op. cit.) McDonald found that where high ceruloplasmin levels were characteristic of a sample of diagnosed schizophrenics it could be completely accounted for by a dietary deficiency of ascorbic acid.

44.  See A. A. Boulton, op. cit. pp. 25-26

45.  F. O. Kelsey *et al* 'Thyroid Activity in Hospitalised Psychiatric Patients' *A.M.A. Archives of Neurology and Psychiatry,* Vol. 77 (1957)

46.  S. S. Kety *et al* 'Cerebral Blood Flow and Metabolism in Shizophrenia' *American Journal of Psychiatry* vol. 104 (1948) and W. P. Wilson *et al* 'Effect of Series of Electro-shock Treatments on Cerebral Blood Flow and Metabolism' *A.M.A. Archives of Neurology and Psychiatry* vol. 68 (1952)

47.   Manfred Bleuler 'Some Results of Research in Schizophrenia,' *Behavioural Science* vol. 15 No. 3 (May 1970) p. 214

48.   Alan A. Boulton, op. cit., p. 27

49.   A. K. Schapiro, 'An Attempt to Demonstrate a Catatonigenic Agent in Cerebrospinal Fluid of Catatonic Schizophrenic Patients' *Journal of Nervous and Mental Disorders* Vol. 123 (1956). Gjessing's findings on the rare and highly specifiable condition of intermittent akinesis ('periodic catatonia') must not be confused with the other forms grouped under the 'syndrome' of 'catatonia' or 'catatonic schizophrenia', for which there exist no nomothetic explanations. Gjessing found that the recurrence of akinesis was correlated highly with periodic malfunctioning of nitrogen metabolism, and the disorder is now known as 'Gjessing's syndrome'.

50.   Brendan Maher *Principles of Psychopathology: An Experimental Approach* McGraw-Hill (1966) p. 354. It is perhaps worth noting Maher's overall conclusion on the organic studies: ' . . . the crucial linkage between histopathology and psychopathology cannot be made on the basis of the evidence so far available' (p. 346), and nothing that has happened in the field since then has altered matters.

51.   Citation from David Rosenthal 'The Heredity-Environment Issue in Schizophrenia: Summary of . . . the Present Status of Our Knowledge' in D. Rosenthal & S. S. Kety (eds.) *The Transmission of Schizophrenia* Pergamon Press (1968) p. 10. Rosenthal makes his own claims in concluding the collaborative work in which he was involved, reported in the same volume.

52.   Manfred Bleuler 'A Twenty-three Year Longitudinal Study of 208 Schizophrenics and Impressions in Regard to the Nature of Schizophrenia' in D. Rosenthal & S. S. Kety (eds.) op. cit. p. 6 et seq

53.   Harry Stack Sullivan *The Psychiatric Interview* Tavistock (1955) p. 207

54.   N. Cameron 'Reasoning, Regression and Communication in Schizophrenics' in Max Hamilton (ed.) *Abnormal Psychology* Penguin (1967) pp. 163-64

55.   L. J. Chapman 'Confusion of Figurative and Literal Usages of Words by Schizophrenics and Brain-Damaged Patients' *Journal of Abnormal and Social Psychology* vol. 60 No. 3 (1960) pp. 412-16

56.   Moyra Williams *Brain Damage and the Mind* Penguin (1970). 'Speech is disturbed in psychiatric patients as well as those with focal cerebral lesions but in general the psychotic speech disorders can be distinguished from those due to focal cerebral lesions' (p. 100). Williams is not *here* claiming that psychotic speech peculiarities can be precisely mapped, but that generally they are different to those *typically* found in brain-damaged subjects. This excellent little book gathers together some of the best recent research in the field.

57.   H. Weil-Malherbe; paper in *Adv. Enzymol.* vol. 29 (1967); cited in A. A. Boulton, op. cit.

58.   C. Rosenbaum; paper in *Journal of Nervous and Mental Disorders* vol. 146 (1968); cited in Boulton

59.   A. R. Kaplan in *Nature* vol. 210 (1966)

60. R. J. Baldessarini & S. H. Snyder in *Nature* vol. 206 (1965)

61. F. J. Kallman 'The Genetic Theory of Schizophrenia: An Analysis of 691 Schizophrenic Twin Index Families' *American Journal of Psychiatry* vol. 103 (1946); F. J. Kallman *Heredity in Health and Mental Disorder* New York, Norton (1953)

62. D. D. Jackson 'A Critique of the Literature on the Genetics of Schizophrenia' in D. D. Jackson (ed.) *The Aetiology of Schizophrenia* Basic Books (1960)

63. Manfred Bleuler 'Some Results of Research in Schizophrenia' op. cit. p. 216

64. L. S. Penrose 'Propagation of Unfit' *The Lancet,* vol. 2 (1950)

65. Bernard Rimland 'Psychogenesis versus Biogenesis: The Issues and the Evidence' in Stanley C. Plog & Robert B. Edgerton (eds.) *Changing Perspectives in Mental Illness* Holt, Rinehart & Winston (1969) pp. 702-35

66. ibid p. 708

67. I. S. Ross 'An Autistic Child' *Pediatric Conferences* (United Hospitals of Newark, New Jersey) vol. 2 No. 2 (1959), pp. 1-13

68. N. Malamud 'Heller's Disease and Childhood Schizophrenia' *American Journal of Psychiatry* vol. 116 (1959) pp. 215-20 (Biochemical and neurological screening remains a pragmatic affair within psychiatric institutions.)

69. B. Rimland op. cit. p. 708

70. Jan. A. Böök 'Genetical Aspects of Schizophrenic Psychoses' in D. D. Jackson (ed.) op. cit.

71. This notion is developed in Warren Torgerson's book *Theory and Method of Scaling* John Wiley (1958), esp. pp. 21-2, and is taken up by Aaron V. Cicourel *Method and Measurement in Sociology* Free Press, Glencoe (1964) Chapter One. Cicourel's methodological discussion is an important resource for some of the ideas developed in *this* chapter.

72. F. J. Kallman 'The Genetic Theory of Schizophrenia . . .' op. cit.

73. D. D. Jackson 'A Critique of the Literature on the Genetics of Schizophrenia . . .' op. cit.

74. E. Essen-Moller 'Psychiatrische Untersuchungen an einer Serie von Zwillingen' *Acta Psychiat. & Neurol.* Supp. 23 (1941) in D. D. Jackson, ibid p. 62

75. W. Pollin, J. R. Stabenau & J. Tupin 'Family Studies with Identical Twins Discordant for Schizophrenia' *Psychiatry: Journal for the Study of Interpersonal Processes* vol. 28 (1965) pp. 119-132

76. Pekka Tienari *Psychiatric Illness in Identical Twins* Copenhagen Munksgaard (1963) and his 'Schizophrenia in Monozygotic Male Twins' in D. Rosenthal & S. S. Kety (eds.) op. cit. pp. 27-36

77. Irving I. Gottesman 'Severity-Concordance and Diagnostic Refinement in the Maudsley-Bethlem Schizophrenic Twin Study' in Rosenthal & Kety op. cit. pp. 37-48

78. Einar Kringlen 'An Epidemiological-Clinical Twin Study on Schizophrenia' in ibid pp. 49-63

79. David Rosenthal op. cit. p. 416. Rosenthal is here expounding one view put forward by some hereditarians; he is not necessarily one of

its proponents

80. L. S. Penrose op. cit. (note 64)

81. Manfred Bleuler 'A Twenty-three Year Longitudinal Study of 208 Schizophrenics...,' op. cit. p. 10

82 Erving Goffman *Asylums: Essays on the Social Situation of Mental Patients and Other Inmates* Doubleday-Anchor New York, (1961)

83. Merton J. Kahne 'Bureaucratic Structure and Impersonal Experience in Mental Hospitals' in S. K. Weinberg (ed.) *The Sociology of Mental Disorders: Analyses and Readings in Psychiatric Sociology* London, Staples Press (1968) pp. 201 et seq

84. J. H. Weakland 'Schizophrenia: Basic Problems in Sociocultural Investigation' in S. C. Plog & R. B. Edgerton (eds.) op. cit. p. 689

85. S. S. Kety *et al* 'The Types and Prevalence of Mental Illness in the Biological and Adoptive Families of Adopted Schizophrenics' in D. Rosenthal & S. S. Kety (eds.) op. cit. pp. 345-62 and David Rosenthal *et al.* 'Schizophrenics' Offspring reared in Adoptive Homes' in ibid pp. 377-91

86. ibid

87. David Rosenthal 'A Program of Research on Heredity in Schizophrenia' *Behavioural Science* vol. 16 No. 3 (May 1971) pp. 191-201

88. Leon Eisenberg 'The Interaction of Biological and Experiential Factors in Schizophrenia' in Rosenthal & Kety (eds.) op. cit. p. 405

89. S. S. Kety *et al* op. cit., p. 360

90. T. Lidz, cited in Rosenthal's summary, in Rosenthal & Kety (eds.) op. cit. note 12 pp. 424-5

91. A. R. Louch *Explanation and Human Action* Oxford, Basil Blackwell (1966) p. 55

92. Bernard Rimland 'Psychogenesis versus Biogenesis: The Issues and the Evidence' in S. C. Plog & R. B. Edgerton (eds.) op. cit. p. 729

93. ibid p. 724. Rimland's paper contains other contradictory assertions. He notes that 'it is indeed true, as many proponents of the psychogenic view have argued, that there are hardly two informed people who agree on what schizophrenia is in general, or on whether or not a given patient is schizophrenic' (p. 719), but also suggests that those disorders recognised and sanctioned in very primitive African societies coincide 'in detail' with 'what we call schizophrenia' (p. 719). If what we call schizophrenia differs between any two informed observers or theoreticians, then this last statement becomes meaningless. (This criticism should not, obviously, be taken to imply that I am leaping to the defence of psychogenesis in any of its forms). However, as one reads Rimland's article and some of his incisive attacks on the woolly thinking in sociogenic and psychogenic frameworks of explanation, a sense of contrast is created in which the biogeneticists appear in a much more favourable light than they would on my reading of their contributions to date. Rimland reserves an aside for some of Skinner's excesses and suggests that his book, *The Behaviour of Organisms* should be retitled *Some Behaviour of Some Organisms*. In the same vein, I should like to retitle Rimland's paper: '...*Some* Issues and *Some* Evidence'. I deal with sociogenic and psychogenic theorizing

in my following chapter, and both there and in the present chapter I have quite deliberately restricted myself to a schematic overview within which some of the basic assumptions and orienting ideals of psychopathologic work can be exposed and assessed.

# CHAPTER TWO

# Schizophrenia as an Experiential Product

*'The result of (sociogenic theories) ... has been almost superstitious belief in a mysterious phenomenon that produces mental disease through personal contact.'* (F. J. Kallman and J. S. Mickey)[1]

*'There is a very real sense in which the schizophrenia problem and the problem of alienation and estrangement in families are identical.'* (David Cooper)[2]

Aetiologists who search for the cause(s) of the schizophrenias in the environments of people who become diagnosed as such are rarely interested in the physico-chemical environments of these people. They focus upon the environment of social relationships. This environment is constituted by communicative interaction; it is, one could say, a *symbolic* environment. In order to get clear of the confusions surrounding the use of 'environment', I prefer to discuss the work of the non-organic aetiologists in terms of investigations into the *experiential* biographies and situations of 'schizophrenics'. The presentations of people who become labelled as 'schizophrenic', in all their variety, are claimed to be the resultants of particular sorts of life experiences. We shall see as the chapter progresses that the locus of these life experiences, supposed to be critical in the genesis of the schizophrenias, is widely taken to be the person's family.

Philosophers of action have often pointed out that in relating someone's conduct to his social situation we are normally engaged in justifying or excusing such conduct. We see that a person is acting, in context, in a certain way and explain it with reference to the contextual particulars of the situation or the person's history, but in doing so we are not providing a *causal* account; rather, we are seeking out those normal conventions that provide for the activity as an intelligible activity, as one which the agent is *entitled* to perform in the given circumstances. In the behavioural sciences, we would often try to convert accounts of conduct into causal ones in which we formulate a set of conditions and then predict that such and such a line of conduct *will* be adopted by a person when those conditions obtain. Now the latter endeavour (sometimes called a 'deductive-nomological' approach) is not currently very popular in the human sciences other than psychopathology, and I think that there are good reasons why it should be suspended there as well. *In giving causal accounts* (or causal-probabilistic ones) *we are converting the agent into the equivalent of an object and proposing that a mechanical, rather than a moral, order of explanation is appropriate.* It is sometimes argued that people who are hospitalised as schizophrenics *are,* in some literal sense, automata to whom the moral vocabulary of action explanations is unfitted. Yet that approach which aims to give some causal account of the patient's current state in terms of antecedent social experiences involves explaining how a sane person *became* an insane one, and as such it must involve reference to the sort of experiences and reactions that this sometime sane person (or perhaps *any* sane person) must be assumed to have endured or participated in himself. Social situations provide grounds or warrants for types of conduct, but not determinants. They permit us or require us to do certain things, and they figure in excusing, justifying and entitling explanations of ordinary conduct. The relevant background of human action is a *moral* background, and not anything like a field of physical occurrences (although physical occurrences are obviously *components* of action and communication). If we propose that a person is insane because of his family's obsessive, irresponsible or threatening treatment of him, we are fixing the locus of responsibility onto the family's members and not formulating a set of necessary and sufficient antecedent conditions for insanity. We are undoubtedly in agreement that the social world contains some awful, traumatic, disorienting, oppressive and confusing circumstances, but whilst our accounts are clear enough as lay accounts when restricted to contexts, they become uselessly vague and inapposite when we attempt to stretch them to cover an entire range of conduct (e.g. insanity) as part of some 'scientific' account. Our ordinary, commonsense explanations of insanity, wherever we give explanations that make reference to features of interpersonal relations and experience, are tied to circumstances, are context-bound; they are *ad hoc* conventional ascriptions of responsibility and the like. But to hope to convert them into generalised theory—generalised aetiological theory, in our case—is to hope in vain. *It is to espouse a programme which illicitly construes the human social world in non-moral terms, on the model of a field of interacting particles or interdeterminate systemic attributes, and it can lead very easily to the apportionment of blame in the guise of scientific explanation.*

The most familiar of the causal accounts is that which reduces the process of human socialisation to the level of animal conditioning; a simple over-extrapolation of Pavlovian reflexology to the normative order of human life experience and interaction. Conditioning theory has never flourished in psychopathology, apart from the early work of Meyer[3] and the occasional use of behaviouristic epistemology for rationalising certain kinds of therapeutic regimes.[4] Eysenck's contributions have remained largely restricted to the 'neuroses',[5] and need not concern us here.

There are many studies of an aetiological type which seek to establish connections between the specific presentations of subjects labelled schizophrenic and specific dimensions of those patterns of interaction that describe the social milieu within which the patient was intermeshed. Inherent in such research is the assumption of what we shall call *pattern introjection;* the internalisation of patterns of family interaction as rules of conduct on the part of the patient. In other words, following Mishler and Waxler, such research is predicated on the view that ' . . . there must be some form of correspondence between the descriptions of interaction patterns and the schizophrenic process if the former are to be aetiologically related to the latter.'[6] Such an approach suggests that some (or all?) 'schizophrenic' patients have learnt uncritically to act and communicate on the basis of instrumentally invalid and culturally deviant modes of family existence; their familial experiences have 'inculcated' into them habits of paralogical thinking, rules of comportment etc, which ill-equip them to carry on a normal life in the wider community. What we have, then, is a socialisation model with its attendant norm of the 'conformity presupposition' (the introjections are blind and unquestioning) in which the subject is moulded and manipulated by a pathological family. It is an essentially commonsensical perspective, with moral and ascriptive properties, put forward in aetiological terms.

T. Lidz and his colleagues have illustrated what they call *the transmission of irrationality* within family units.[7] In a series of papers, Lidz and his colleagues concentrated exclusively upon intrafamilial relationships, leaving aside the family members' larger social networks, and reported that in the cases of fifteen subjects diagnosed as schizophrenic at the Yale Psychiatric Institute the families of those schizophrenics had constructed over the years highly idiosyncratic microcultures within which these subjects had been reared. The idiosyncracies were stated to have been 'pathogenic', and consisted in the inculcation and acceptance of distorted interpretations of reality. Moreover, two forms of 'pathogenic' family structure were evaluated : 'marital schism' and 'marital skew'. In the schismatic family structure, there were 'severe chronic disequilibrium and discord . . . recurrent threats of separation . . . . Communication consists of coercive efforts and defiance, or of efforts to mask the defiance to avoid fighting. There is little or no sharing of problems or satisfactions . . . chronic 'undercutting' of the worth of one partner to the children by the other [takes place]. The tendency for competition for the children's loyalty and affection is prominent . . . . Mutual distrust of motivations is the rule.'[8] In skewed family structures, Lidz and his associates see one marital partner dominating the home and manifesting idiosyncratic or unusual beliefs about himself or the world which are voiced only within the family. In the families studied, 'facts are constantly being altered to suit emotionally determined needs. The children learn that meanings are not primarily in the service of reality testing . . . . The acceptance of mutually contradictory experiences requires paralogical thinking. Such environments provide training in irrationality.'[9] The result is that children reared in such families learn to detach themselves easily from the practical demands of the outer culture and their family experiences have taught them that communication of fact and experience can be highly precarious to their emotional stability.

Much of what Lidz and his associates describe might well be found to fit quite ordinary families whose members have never seen psychiatric specialists of any kind, and there are several passages above in which mundane occurrences are accorded quite extraordinary significance; even in the most close interpersonal bond, communication of commands and efforts to get the partner to do as one wishes can be found along with related attempts to suppress defiance in order to avoid a row; 'facts' are regularly being matched to people's needs and relevances—indeed, there are no 'neutral' facts about interpersonal dealings, only facts constituted as such through moral, negotiated interactions. This last point can also be extended to cover Lidz's problem with 'distorted interpretations of reality'; we are not told there exactly what order of interpretations were being fostered or avowed within the families, but there is clearly a tendency to erect the researcher's view of 'reality' as a standard by which to assess the interpretations of others.

We are provided with fragments of data to support these generalized contentions. We are asked to 'see' the fragments as evidences of pathogenic family relationships. In effect, we are being asked to join Lidz and his colleagues in finding in the data 'good grounds' for the patients' current predicaments, grounds which were not forthcoming from the patients themselves nor ascribed to them by official and unofficial personnel responsible for their diagnosis and hospitalization. But the rhetoric of this approach constrains us to ask for some 'model' of routine family functioning and socializ-ation practices and for some attempt at statistical evaluation of the 'results'. It is as if we need telling what correct, expectable and routine family life is like in order for us to be persuaded that Lidz *et al* are isolating pathogenic variables. The whole conception of a 'variable' belongs to a different order of theory and research than that involved with social process and communication, and the con-cept of 'pathogenicity' fits poorly with work on non-biological data. The enterprise is best read, I would argue, as an attempt to scientise what amount to a set of commonsense cultural judgments.

There are additional, purely methodological, grounds for scepti-cism about the Lidz studies. 1. The family is accorded the status of solitary agency for child socialisation for practical research purposes, and there is no way of knowing what checks on the children's behavi-our obtained outside the family unit (e.g. amongst peer groups at school and elsewhere). The family is seen too much as a total institu-tion, hermetically sealed off from the 'reality-testing', often cruel and earthy, which goes on in the street, school and playing field. 2. The assumption pervades the research programme that there is an isomorphism of relevances between researcher(s) and emergent patient. That is, it is supposed that the researcher's reading of various situations, his attribution of significance to varieties of family interaction, is in a close correspondence to that of the index case. Of course, what the researcher is doing is using his commonsense knowledge of what would *entitle* or *provoke* certain kinds of conduct in a child as a resource for interpreting the events he witnesses. 3. Patients' own definitions of their familial situation are rarely available (since quite often the patient does not communicate in a comprehensible manner) and thus cannot be used as checks on the reliability of a researcher's definitions. 4. Interactional events, styles and patterns of communication and relationship are assessed *after* the election and eviction of the index case whose 'schizophrenia' prompts the aetiological research in the first place. The result is that observations obtained ex post facto are accorded *aetiological* significance.[10] It remains almost impossible to 'control for' the possibility that any disorganisation of the family of a 'schizophrenic' is the result of, rather than the 'cause' or reason for, the disorder of that particular family member.

The family interaction studies[11] grew out of a despondency with the prevalent unifactor models in psychopathology, such as the 'isolation hypothesis', the 'schizophrenigenic mother' explanation, the 'broken homes' account[12] and other such constructions where only one extrapolated variable was correlated to diagnosed index cases. I want to say something at this point about the practice of operationalization, and especially the construction of 'variables', and then to move on to a brief discussion of the ecological and epidemiological approaches to the problem of social causation of insanity (schizophrenia and related 'functional' disorders).

Many facts about social phenomena, such as sex, age and income distributions, organizational affiliation figures and voting patterns can be formulated as 'variables', as quantitative indices, with little more than commonsense computations and ingenuity. The physical and biological facts about a society can be counted and measured quite literally. However, when complex orders of human activity, such as those which enter into the phenomena of business depressions, social integration, birth control programmes and the like, are construed as 'variables', theoretical problems loom large. Herbert Blumer, in his paper on variable analysis,[13] noted that for such cases the empirical reference is neither unitary nor distinct : 'When caught in its actual social character, [the variable] turns out to be an intricate and inner-moving complex.'[14] Further, the attempt to relate fields of action construed in terms of dependent and independent variables assumes that the independent variable (which is after all a sociologist's construct) emanates its own fixed, intrinsic and universal meaning or significance for people. Blumer goes on to remark that people *confer* significance or relevance on objects, events and situations, and such a practice is essentially interpretational; but one cannot transform the 'act of interpretation' itself into an 'intervening variable' between the independent and dependent ones, since interpretations are hardly neutral media through which the independent variables exercise their influence or achieve predetermined effects. Blumer highlights the problem with an example that is well suited for his purposes. He outlines a typical sort of variable-analytic study in which an already given quantitative index, the birth rate of a particular locality, is related to a qualitative, 'processual' phenomenon, a programme of birth control, and the aim of the study is taken to be that of ascertaining the *influence* of the latter on the former. Normal practice in the cases of processual variables is to treat quantifiable facts about them as 'indicators' of them, so that the birth control programme could be 'measured' in terms of the number of people visiting birth control clinics. Blumer notes that a simple scrutiny of what the two variables actually stand for in terms of how they enter into the lives of people reveals the need for much more data. One has to know something about the literacy of the people, the clarity of the circulated information, the scope of its distribution, how the birth control programme personnel interact with the recipients of their programme, the ways in which people define attendance at clinic sessions, etc. On the other hand, the apparently more straightforward birth rate index cannot stand on its own—one must supplement it with data on the variety of social factors that impinge on the conduct and frequency of the sexual act, the values placed on children, the accessibility of mates, etc, all of which are expressed in the birth rate that is registered for the locality. The variable relationship arrived at will simply pare down such information and will therefore assert a spurious connection between 'abbreviated terms of reference'.[15]

The classical epidemiological studies in psychopathology, amongst which one could number those of Hollingshead and Redlich,[16] Faris and Dunham,[17] Srole and his collaborators,[18] Pasamanick[19] and Clausen,[20] were patterned on the model of demography. Not all were involved in making statements about ecological relationships that had an aetiological significance, although there is often a strong suggestion that findings about rates of processed mental disorder and their correlation with other social phenomena such as social class position (operationally scaled) 'imply' findings pertaining to causality of mental disorder. However, as Dunham has more recently noted :

> If he (the ecologist) tries to get at the social factors that are causative or predisposing for persons in [the] environment, he will be thrown on another level of analysis where his ecological findings will prove only indicative of some factors that he might study as having aetiological significance.[21]

Frequently, the studies of epidemiologists have been cited as the basis for speculative theorizing about the ways in which the 'variables' or 'social factors' related in their studies actually work themselves out 'on the ground' (i.e. in daily experience) as causally efficient in the production of e.g. schizophrenia. It is assumed that the trends postulated from the aggregate data to be in operation hold in constant fashion for each particular incident or case. Furthermore, it has been proposed that epidemiological studies do not study a pristine 'rate of schizophrenia', but rather the extent to which family and/or community members shelter or eject their deviant members.[22] The idea that there is a 'real rate' lurking *behind* the ascription practices of members of a community in particular or a society at large, to which members are only differentially *responsive,* omits the important consideration that any type of insanity is constituted as such only in the context of practical interactions and their attendant ordinary judgemental processes. Any rate is as real as the practical judgments and coding apparatus of a given mental health 'area' can produce. If one presses some other criteria for the 'reality' of a given rate, one rapidly ends up substituting one's own research judgments for those of a rate-producing community or official psychiatric agency. I think that this furnished the basis for the Srole metropolitan study; here, an attempt was made to determine the distribution of persons in a community manifesting 'psychiatric symptoms' or 'illness' who had *not* applied for psychiatric assistance or been referred to a psychiatric facility.[23] Srole and his colleagues found that 23.4% of the population studied were 'suffering' from various types of 'psychiatric disorder' and only 18% were symptom free ! Instead of accepting the rhetoric of the study, which made great play of the 'discovery' of a large amount of insanity being 'contained' by the society, one can read it as a sustained, unilateral imputation of mental disorder to people on the basis of undisclosed interactional experiences with them and the application of a predefined set of ascription rules in undisclosed ways.

I do not want to develop a discussion of epidemiology here; there are naturally many practical advantages (for planning and policy-making) in having such studies. What I have suggested, however, with respect to the question of non-organic aetiological research, is that such studies cannot provide a basis for inferences of an aetiological sort.

As I noted earlier, the unifactor studies of insanity, to which one can add the multiple correlation studies of some ecologists, have not satisfied the nomothetic impulse of the causal theorists in psycho-pathology. The shift of focus to processes of social interaction marked the beginnings of a sustained attempt at generating aetiological theories which sought to explain the phenomena of insanity (especially schizophrenic psychoses) in the most direct terms, starting out from the detailed investigation of individual cases and then extrapolating to other cases. The recurrent problem in such work has been the tendency to rather abstract and formal specifi-cations which create great difficulty for replication : given a very abstract and formal description, what can and cannot count as a legitimate set of observables within its frame of reference? Attempt-ing to remove as many contextual particularities as possible from the individual case interaction processes leaves behind only a vague and loose formulation which has to be concretised again in some other set of circumstances of interaction if it is to serve as a general theory covering many cases. It is the move to reconcretize the abstract formulations of the interactionist researchers which proves especially troublesome. Their conceptual foci, also, differ so markedly that cumulativity in theory construction has remained unattained.

The perspective developed by Lyman C. Wynne and his colleagues[24] centred upon the very abstract conception of 'pseudo-mutuality' in family interaction processes. This made reference to the alleged suppression of communicative reciprocity in the family units of diagnosed schizophrenics. The differentiation of a personal identity or distinct individuality on the part of a family member was considered impossible in such families because of the consistent use of interpersonal techniques by members that prohibited or strongly sanctioned the articulation of such individuality or personal independence within any interactional episode. Wynne and his colleagues claimed that no independent expectations of any sort were allowed or tolerated within the family units studied, and communications geared to the presentation of conflicting demands, or divergent perspectives to those established in the past by parents, became diffused, blurred or hopelessly distorted. This conception was entirely within the pattern-introjection model of aetiological theorising noted earlier in connection with the work of Lidz *et al;* as Wynne put it,

> ... the fragmentation of experience, the identity diffusion, the disturbed modes of perception and communication, and certain other characteristics of the acute reactive schizophrenic's personality structure are to a significant extent derived, by processes of internalisation, from characteristics of the family social organisation.[25]

Since several of my criticisms of the conceptual and method-ological basis of the Lidz studies seem to apply to Wynne and his colleagues, I shall not repeat them here. In this discussion, I want to consider the issue of adducing relatively context-independent descriptions of human interaction as integral features of aetiological theory.

The Wynne study leaves us with the question of how to go about identifying 'pseudo-mutuality', or even its indicators, such as an absence of 'communicative reciprocity,' intolerance of independent expectations, and the like, in other cases in such a way that would satisfy the Wynne group's criteria of adequate recognition *and* enable us to claim either (a) that in *our* researches such phenomena were located or (b) that we were unable to locate such phenomena. If we cannot make identifications separately from Wynne's group, then we can never be in any position either to validate or refute their claims. Although Wynne and his colleagues stipulate that their 'clinical examples are included for illustration and clarification, not for statistical verification,'[26] it is assumed that any independent team of researchers will find it a straightforward matter to register some set of events as the 'same' as or 'equivalent' to those appraised in the paradigm study. However, no observer of some social situation or series of situations can warrantably suppose that his appraisals would be concurred in by all parties to those situations : aetiological models of a sociological type demand that the subject has made the same (kind of) assessment of intra-familial situations as the researcher, and has developed styles of conduct predicated upon routinised understandings of the expectations and levels of tolerance of other family members. It is at this point where we find such an approach unavoidably flawed.

The force of the interactionist approach is largely decided by the success of researchers in so describing and evaluating interpersonal situations that the descriptions and evaluations persuade us to see in what has been described good enough grounds for the particular member's insanity, or clear enough foundations for reconstructing the learning environment of the member. Wynne's group concentrates upon the latter, and as such seeks not so much to persuade us to find in what they describe some conditions that 'would drive Anyone mad,' but rather some conditions that we should think of as liveable-in only if one adopts the style of conduct actually discerned in the ejected, insane member. Yet this raises the problem of why it is that in such families a member whose conduct is predicated upon such a congruent set of maxims, expectations and outlooks should have been found so grossly deviant as to elicit the label of 'psychiatric case,' if not outright 'insanity', from co-members of the same families. One might have thought that someone whose conduct closely matched the group conduct, exactly mirrored the dispositions of other members and appeared even to be shaped by an *internalisation* of their patterns of action, would have been thought of as a conformist—perhaps even a self-effacing conformist —rather than a deviant in their midst.

What social aetiologists describe, or appraise, are episodes in the daily lives of family members, from which inferences about their general modes of social organisation and communication are formulated. But, taken separately, the data amounts to a set of isolates from the flux of experience within the family studied, upon which ad hoc assessments are imposed. There is obviously no way of listing interactional observables as strict correlates of any given appraisal (e.g. 'manifestation of subterfuge,' 'suppression of individuation,' 'contradictory expectations,' etc), since appraisals of social scenes are very different from descriptions or measurements of physical events or physio-chemical reactions. Yet I believe that a notion of natural-scientific description underpins the social aetiologist's attempts : what such theorizing attains is commonsense appraisal in the guise of scientific generality. In our ordinary affairs as members of a society, we make ascriptions, imputations and appraisals of members, their situations, and the 'fit' between the two, but we do so within a framework of practical interests and contingencies and under the auspices of some conception of the here and now. When such practical ascriptions and appraisals are elevated to the status of scientific theory and divorced from practical, situated interchanges, ordinary standards of adequacy and the possibility of routine rebuttal and argument vanish, along with the specific contextual particulars that ground the appraisals in the first place, and we are left with a curious amalgam of ad hoc observations, unilateral selections of criterial events and processes, arbitrary ascription and imputation and a technical expression of such an amalgam.

Studies like those of Lidz and Wynne and their colleagues replace a conception of an insane person's self-presentations as disease symptoms with a conception of them as learnt social deviances, acquired almost exclusively from intrafamilial experiences. We do not require the interactionist focus on families to agree with their insistence upon the need for a reconceptualization of insanity, however. As I have tried to argue, there are no good reasons for believing that each and every case of insanity is a case of disease, and that what we see the insane person doing and talking about is solely the uncontrolled product of a brain malfunction. But if a person is agreed to be insane (whatever the disagreement about the precise nature or form of his insanity), then it is agreed that what he says and does is, for the most part, inexplicable by reference to culturally available standards of speech and conduct relative to the person's social role or social identity. No amount of searching in the biography of the person can come up with any consideration that would enable us to comprehend his current situation, or, if it does, then we would surely be tempted to alter our view of the person as insane in the first place. (We would perhaps say that he is 'after all' doing what he is doing *for a reason,* and a reason that entitles him to do what he is doing—therefore, although *we* might not behave that way, it is apparent why *he* feels the need to do so.) I should like to postpone further discussion of the logic of members' ascription practices until later chapters. I want to move to a consideration of a very influential approach to schizophrenia within the sociogenic perspective : that of the Bateson team.[27]

The 'Double Bind' Theory of Schizophrenia pioneered by Gregory

Bateson and his collaborators was based upon the formal analysis of social processes within which the diagnosed schizophrenic person was located. Bateson, an anthropologist by training, developed the theoretical architecture of his approach to insanity out of some research he undertook in New Guinea in the '30s. At that time, the occidental government of New Guinea, spurred on by missionaries, were objecting to the transvestite practices of the native population. These practices appeared to play a positive role in the culture of that population in neutralising any potentially disruptive sexual rivalry. The demands of the government faced the New Guineans with one of two equally appalling prospects; either the extermination of their culture from without, or the commencement of internal disruption of unknown severity from within. Irrespective of the teleological functionalism inherent in ascribing some overall goal to particular cultural practices apart from the avowals of the native practitioners, the study did furnish an important sociological notion of contradiction—a social situation of 'can't win either way' —which came to be conceptualized later as a 'double-bind' situation. Bateson and his colleagues elaborated the formal structure of double bind situations as a basis for a theory of the genesis of disorganised thought and speech characteristic of many diagnosed schizophrenics. In their 1956 paper, they proposed the following schema : the necessary ingredients for a pathogenic double bind situation were seen to be (1) two or more people, (2) repeated experience, (3) primary negative injunction enforced with threats of sanction, (4) secondary injunction conflicting with the first at a more abstract level and accompanied, like the first, with signals threatening survival, (5) a tertiary injunction prohibiting escape from the intercommunicative field, and finally (6) the stage is attained where the victim perceives his universe of social relations in double bind patterns, and the entire interactional ingredients are no longer necessary. Let us consider some examples. A mother beckons to her child and tells him that he must not keep running home to her every time he gets into fights with his playmates in the street or at school, but then states that he is to treat the home as a refuge, as a place where he can always unburden himself of any problems and that this is expected of him. Then the child is instructed to concur with these remarks. Another example, this time of conflicting *positive* injunctions, might be where a mother tells her child to approach and kiss her, but paralinguistically demonstrates acute distaste at the impending close physical contact, whilst further insisting that the child do as she is told, this time with stern severity. Of course, it is assumed that the child, in both cases, perceives the contradictoriness of the messages, and yet since 'survival' is 'threatened', must comply. 'Survival' is a rather odd term here, since it remains unclear whether what is intended by the term is the survival, or continuance, of the interactional episode itself, or the emotional bonds between the interactants, or the maintenance of the family's social relationships as a whole. A further specification of the constituents of double binds is given in the same paper. This involves (1) a relationship in which one subject considers it vitally important that his presentation of himself is pleasing to others and thence feels it essential to discriminate properly what is communicated to him, (2) where two orders of message are being transmitted, one conflicting with the other, and (3) the individual is constrained against commenting upon the messages being transmitted in order to correct his discrimination of what order to respond to. In this formulation, an affective dimension is incorporated into the elements of the schema. However, the notion of communicative levels remains abstruse. Polarities in communicative form which have predominantly been stressed by these theorists include the 'abstract/concrete' levels, 'linguistic/paralinguistic', 'communication/metacommunication', 'literal/metaphorical', 'content/role relationship', and 'particularity/context'. Communicative transactions involving disharmonies between such levels are referred to as double-bind transactions. Each of these dichotomies proves immensely troublesome in terms of warrantably locating some items from the flux of communications that might be subsumed under them. The 'contextual' level is prehaps the most troublesome, since referrents for it have differed from 'expectation of outcome' to accounts of the entire environing circumstances including time and place of communication. The whole approach is a classic example of extrapolating formal properties and then having trouble warranting their relocation in other data; by concentrating upon commonsense assertions about the ways in which some people appear to disconfirm an obvious interpretation of what they are saying, the Bateson team give no indication at all about the importance of such a consideration with respect to what it is that is being communicated. It appears from their perspective that, no matter how trivial or mundane, no matter how concrete or innocuous, an utterance or sequence of utterances might seem, if that utterance or sequence can be found to manifest properties of form in accord with double-bind specifications, then a double-bind situation of some degree of pathogenicity has been created.[28]

Schuham's review of the literature on double bind theory[29] makes reference to the objection that, while the theory stipulates that the crucial issue is the participant's perception of the communicative situation in which he finds himself, case records supposed to substantiate the claims of the theory tend to reflect observers' interpretations of what constitute congruent or incongruent messages of various types. It is left undecided whether or not the victim of double-bind communications has to realise that he is a target of them if pathogenicity is to be asserted. Of course, a crucial impasse in treating the theory as a scientific theory to be tested and verified in a positivistic fashion is this : how is one to measure, or otherwise warrantably assess, a subtle communicative process occurring selectively over time in the general transactions of at least two people who are communicating simultaneously on different levels?[30] The absence of agreed procedures for sifting through and evaluating what can count as 'evidence for' the theory and 'evidence against' it has made life difficult for its proponents. Attempts to generalize the theory to three party interactions[31] and the addition of conceptions such as 'split double-bind' and 'quadruple bind' have just clouded the initial formulations and made rigorous assessment of its adequacy more remote. The extension of the theory from 'schizophrenia' to cover such diverse phenomena as delinquency, hypnotic trance induction, enjoyment of play and phantasy, humour and laughter, written communications and psychotherapeutic relationships has not demonstrated any 'intrinsic' merit of the schema, merely its utility as a convenient metaphorical descriptive framework for a wide range of human activities. In that sense, it now makes it impossible to claim that double bind relationships of communication· are pathognomic to the schizophrenias, and one theorist, Watzlawick,[32] has commented : 'indeed, it would be impossible to imagine any emotional involvement, such as for instance courtship, in which double binding does not constitute a core element.' In recent years, then, double-bind theory has declined as a theoretical framework of any importance for experiential aetiology.

I do not intend to ramify the examples of family interaction studies, since we can perhaps agree with the conclusion of Mishler and Waxler :

> They are less like scientific theories than artful constructions or coherent accounts arrived at independently through different perspectives and methods of conceptualization. Their value to other investigators, like that of art, lies in giving us a new way of looking at the world.[33]

The sociological tradition founded on the pragmatist philosophy of George Herbert Mead and called 'symbolic interactionism' (by Blumer,[34] whose work we have already mentioned) has generated a good deal of theory and research in the sociology of deviant activities. The symbolic interactionists have tended to conceptualize their research problems with insanity in two ways. Either they have taken Meadian conceptions of 'self' and 'reflexiveness' as the basic constructs with which to understand the genesis of types of insanity (i.e. a strictly aetiological perspective), or they have treated populations of insane people in mental hospitals as the emergents from complex processes of social typification, status negotiation and other interactional contingencies (i.e. a societal ejection theory of mental hospital members). Manford Kuhn, of the Iowa school of symbolic interactionism, has attempted to specify an operational definition of 'self' which could be used in causal research. In conceiving of the self as a variable, Kuhn wrote that

> The two most frequently compelling questions are : (1) the question whether the self is conceived, for research purposes, as the antecedent variable with criterion events (especially behaviours) as consequent variables, or conversely whether antecedent variables (ascribed identities, affiliations, associations, communication variables and other events) are conceived to predict—that is, exist in regularity with—consequent self-variations; and (2) the question whether the relevant antecedent variables are conceived to be *immediate* or *remote* in time with respect to the events thought of as consequent.[35]

Kuhn delineated nine different variants in the symbolic interactionist literature on the relationship between causal variables and self variations (and this is, incidentally, only one extra variant over the number of conceptions of 'stimulus' prevalent in contemporary psychological theory according to Gibson[36]). It would seem that the problems are fundamentally of the theorists' own devising, since they begin by operationally reifying 'the self' as if it were something apart from or other than those processes within which the person has acted. The result of operationalizing 'self' in this way is that whatever is being placed in a more or less determinate relationship to the other 'variables' Kuhn lists, it bears no necessary relationship to what an actor would stipulate as his conception of himself at any particular time and in any specific context. The temporal problem in relating self-conceptions to other social events arises because the investigator, operating with a unilateral definition of someone's self-conception based on fragmentary interpretations of aspects of his interaction, has trouble in reading off *any* causal relationship between what happens to a person and how he alters his conception of himself. I am not suggesting that this situation can be remedied; I include reference to it because it seems to indicate sharply the conceptual and methodological puzzles that beset any positivistic redefinition of 'self' and 'self-conception'.

Emphasis upon the role of 'self' in human activities stems from a consistent dissatisfaction with zoomorphic, operant conditioning theories of human action and experience. Operantism postulates action as reaction, as unmediated learnt responses to preestablished classes of sensory stimulation. Lacking a notion of symbolisation, operantism fails to conceptualise the organisation of action and interaction as human constructions; instead, it concentrates solely upon the elements of organic behaviour which are employed in social acts, from which it is falsely concluded that, since organic behaviours are either learnt or reflexive, then all action is one of the two. The fact that many human acts are predicated upon complex symbolic processes, such as projection and communication, seemed to call for some notion of an intermediary or intervening principle between stimulus class (however conceived) and response set. Mead saw this principle as the 'self'. The individual is a self-endowed organism, and this meant that it was not tenable to construe him as simply sensitive protoplasm receiving stimulation from without, but as an active agent that sought out and selected stimuli from an array of possibilities of stimulation. Mead construed the human organism as active per se; the direction of activities could not be accounted for by assuming constant and automatic outputs of conditioning. Rather, the individual was to be seen as engaged in a continuous process of interpretation of his environment, a process Mead termed 'self-indication', and it is this process which Mead saw as creating for man a symbolic environment in which objects stand as fields of possibilities for action towards them rather than as fixed loci of stimulation. Relationships between individuals could not be reduced to episodes of inter-stimulation, but had to be thought of as active processes of interindication, i.e. in which each participant indicates something both to himself and the self of the other. Furthermore, intersubjective processes of symbolisation were not seen exclusively as the exchange of *representations* of environing stimuli, but media in which individuals could relate without any immediate reference to the surrounding matrix of sensory stimulation. One can transform, disconnect and project conceptions through symbolisation, as well as use symbols to stand for something in a common perspectival range. Operantism involves treating communication—talking in particular—in terms of fragmented vocal-auditory response series linguistic creativity and the variability of interpretive possibilities are both left unaccounted for. Noam Chomsky has recently criticized a sophisticated version of operantism along these lines.[37] The impulse of operantist accounts of human action and communication seems to be that of wanting to assimilate very diverse phenomena to one kind of explanatory scheme, irrespective of their different logical status.

My digression on the role of the concept of 'self' in the history of the sociological critique of operant conditioning theories of human action is intended as a background against which to assess the contemporary use being made of the notion in aetiological work. It is quite doubtful whether Mead or Dewey would have concurred in the reification of self which underpins some of the Iowa studies, nor in the attempt to see in biographical and historical data on interactional experiences some coercive, causal 'variables' that have putatively acted *upon* someone and conditioned a transformation in their self-conception. Kuhn's 'measurement' of someone's self-conception, prior to an investigation of its 'antecedents', involves getting a subject to respond in twenty different ways to the question, 'Who Am I?'.[38] The results of this Twenty Statements Test are coded as indicators of a person's organization of his attitudes towards himself. It seems unlikely, however, that such a codification actually measures anything; a person arrives at twenty different ways of presenting his identity (usually including items from his social biography, occupational status, physical characteristics and so on) which amount to twenty different articulations of varying relevance to him and of widely diverse relationship to concrete courses of action in which he may engage or have engaged.[39] McPartland and Cumming[40] have utilized the TST in order to postulate general relationships between mental patients' 'self-conceptions' and their clinical diagnoses (on the basis of correlations), and in their collaborative work with W. S. Garretson[41] they attempted to relate TST scores to variations in ward behaviour in mental institutions. The problem with such 'self-construct' studies is similar to the problem with attitudinal studies : both self-conception and attitude define possible tendencies to act, but some knowledge of either in a social situation is not sufficient for us to assert that self-conception or attitude actually direct and shape any given activity. Moreover, neither can be used as predictors of activities. In everyday parlance, terms such as self-conception and attitude refer us less to what someone *will* do and more to the sort of state he is in, and our estimation of the sort of state someone is in derives from inferences from previous observations of his speech and conduct. I can see no way of sharpening up the concepts to yield *harder* information about a person. One can, of course, assume consistencies, but that assumption can be rudely shattered in ordinary dealings with any person in various sorts of situation. Further, I doubt if attempts at sampling social situations or interactions will help matters; the whole idea of sampling events rather than people is an odd one.

In Mead's terminology, the 'self' is nothing other than the reflexiveness of the human organism—Mead used the notion of self to stress the cognitive capacity of humans to reflect upon their own actions, their own faculties and powers, as if they were 'at a distance', so to speak, from their agents. Generally, the human organism acts towards others with the background knowledge that such others are also possessed of the capacity for reflexiveness (this is perhaps what is intended by the notion of the 'self of the other'). Despite some of the unfortunate formulations of his more metaphysical followers, it is clear that Mead intended nothing mysterious in his use of the concept of 'self'. He would quite likely have agreed with Richard Taylor's verdict on much of the 'philosophy of selfhood,' namely that : 'One can, if he likes, say that the ultimate cause of a voluntary bodily motion is a self, but what is this but another way of saying that men sometimes act, or that they are active beings?'[42] To propose that human beings *have* selves may appear to involve 'an odd transformation of grammar'[43] in Taylor's terms, but for Mead all that such a proposition amounted to was a reassertion of the crucial role of reflexiveness in human conduct and its explanations, in contrast to the prevailing dehumanization inherent in the theoretical perspective of Watsonian behaviourism.

One theorist, Ernest Becker, discussing schizophrenia as a form of human alienation, treats 'the self' as the 'sense of being' which humans have, and suggests that the confirmation of a significant sense of being is contingent upon experiences of control and active manipulation of an environment of social objects, whilst alienation is 'the forfeiting of self-powers'. What Becker is placing at the centre of his theoretical framework is the idea of the exercise of human autonomy as the mainspring of an integrated and harmonious self-image. Action undertaken according to one's own self-conceived projects and purposes, according to one's own initiatory powers, is seen as enriching, reinforcing and confirming one's sense of significance, one's awareness of one's dynamic faculties and capabilities in the face of others.[44] Becker seeks to relate a hypothesized deprivation of autonomous action amongst those diagnosed as schizophrenic with the clinical picture some of them present of detachment, derealisation and phantasizing. For Becker, 'schizophrenic passivity is a direct reflex of the abrogation of one's powers in the face of the object'; he continues :

> The object's powers are greater than those of the self.
> If you relate to an object under your own initiatory powers, then it becomes an object which enriches your own nature. If you lack initiatory powers over the object, it takes on a different value, for it then becomes an individuality which crowds your own nature. This is nowhere more patent than in the schizophrenic's self-effacement in a threatening world, where everything has existential priority but himself.[45]

Becker's undifferentiated notion of 'object' inhibits a clear translation of these ideas into concrete examples. In taking out a cigarette and lighting it I could be said to be engaged in initiatory action towards an object, but it seems a little far fetched to suppose that such an object 'enriches' my nature. (By that latter term, I imagine something like 'feelings of significance' or 'sense of autonomy' or 'humanness' might be involved.) Again, there are many objects over which I might have no wish to exercise any control whatsoever (I might be a pacifist who hates weaponry or a Muslim who won't touch alcoholic liquor). Becker must, apparently, be thinking of objects which I want to act towards but cannot for some reason. Yet there are many such objects in a person's world, and it is rather over-speculative to presume that an inability to control them or use them leads to the development of a conception of them as 'crowding' one's 'nature;' people are frequently prepared to forget about the whole thing, to move on to something more tangible, more obtainable, and resignation is scarcely a key factor in invoking or eliciting cognitive confusion. The inability to obtain some valued object rarely leads to a detachment from the world of objects and their pursuance—Becker's phenomenology of self and object seems to presuppose a quite abnormal sort of reaction to mundane experiences. He raises the value we attach to some degree of autonomy as humans to the level of a generic, preoccupying mystique in order to read into the withdrawal of some schizophrenics merely a more 'patent' version of that allegedly routine feeling of domination by alien objects he describes above. In order to 'render intelligible' some aspects of schizophrenic states, he must render unintelligible our ordinary dealings with our environment of others and objects.

From a different tradition, although in a similar vein, D. Bannister's approach to the genesis of schizophrenia draws on the construct theory of personality developed by G. A. Kelly.[46] Bannister presents the idea that those presentations diagnosed as 'thought-disordered' by a clinician and found in some persons considered schizophrenic are in fact the result of a determinable mode of socialisation. This mode involves the persistent (or 'serial' in Bannister's terms) invalidation in practical experience of the conceptions developed by such people to enable them to deal with other people.[47] Due to this experience of serial invalidation of their 'personal constructs,' some people 'loosen' them, refashion them in vague terms, as a mechanism of normalization, and this is held to account for the observation Bannister cites of many classified 'thought-disordered' subjects seeming quite capable of coping with the physical environment of objects (their naming, manipulation, etc) whilst at the same time their attitudes towards, and functioning with, other people seems grossly uncoordinated. As Bannister and Salmon put it, we can often observe such people 'confidently handling doors, cutlery and shoelaces but failing entirely to distinguish friend from foe'.[48] This reiterates my earlier point about symptomatological discontinuities, and there are many clinical profiles that support such a perspective. Two examples can briefly be given. The first is an observation by Lidz and his colleagues :

> ... the irrationality [can tend to] become more or less circum-scribed. This girl who writes violently invective letters filled with delusions to her parents will in the next minute write a letter to a friend without a trace of delusional material, and then sits in her room and correctly composes inordinately complex music. No defect of thinking due to dysfunction of the brain permits such highly organised conceptualization.[49]

The second example is taken from a paper by Fleck,[50] in which he describes a man preoccupied with strange mystical religions and who looked like the Messiah :

> As if this appearance were not bizarre enough in the setting of an unbelievably messy room in which he hoarded food, a typical daily scene showed him almost naked, sitting on his toilet, study-ing stock quotations in the *Wall Street Journal.* It may be noted in passing that he showed a typically schizophrenic phenomenon, exhibiting severe psychotic and delusional behaviour, unable to have any comfortable human contact, while still able to select a stock portfolio for his therapist that he predicted correctly would increase 40% on the market in a year's time—a coexistence of abnormal and normal high-order mentation never encountered in any known organic brain disorder.[51]

The issue seems to me to call for a revision of the total disease model of insanity ('the schizophrenias'), and, as Bannister and Salmon suggest, any account of 'causal processes,' particularly organic ones, 'may legitimately be asked to account for a differential degree of thought disorder in different construct subsystems'.[52] However, as we saw in the citation from Lidz *et al* above, the differential occurrence of peculiar, unreasonable conduct is not stratified strictly along the social/physical dimensions, as their young girl appeared to restrict her bizarre expressions to her parents, and not to all and sundry personal acquaintances. Once more, the nomothetic impulse has to be checked. A further problem is that there is no way of determining the necessary extent of 'construct invalidation' that is supposed to occur (or have occurred) in the everyday existence of Bannister's subjects, nor is there any clear indication of the types of invalidation thought most deleterious, nor the sort of persons thought likely to be most significantly involved in whatever invalidations take place. The ad hoc device of postulat-ing the normalization mechanism to take such a peculiar form as the 'loosening' of personal constructs becomes elevated to the status of a theory of anxiety avoidance, but this is hardly satisfactory, as the gap between a sane and an insane response to such 'invalidatory' experiences remains unbridged by such a theory. Anxiety can surely be avoided in more rational ways than by presenting oneself as a confused and thought-disordered person. Frequently, theories such as this which seek to explain aspects of insane performances assume quite insane sorts of responses or conceptualizations in the first place, and then move on to consider some range of phenomena that might have been so responded to or so conceptualized. For the family interaction students, such phenomena were certain sorts of intra-familial experiences construed as 'psychonoxious' (I do not incorporate *all* of the family studies in this assessment); for the double bind theorists, such phenomena comprised series of contradictory messages (which 'produced' subjects' refusals to be responsible for the metacommunicative dimensions of their utterances and hence their peculiarities of conduct); for Becker, the phenomena were unattainable or uncontrollable objects, and for Bannister and his associates, the phenomena are experiences of serial invalidation of ideas about other people.

The ease with which post hoc sociogenic or psychogenic explanations can be found in the social biographies of diagnosed schizophrenics should lead us be somewhat sceptical of 'discoveries' in the field of experiential aetiology. There is little reason to suppose that whatever peculiarity (in our terms) we can come up with after digging into a patient's past is either causally efficient in 'producing' his 'disease' or an instance of some generally determinate causal agency in cases of diagnosed schizophrenia. We might, of course, seek to interpret some past occurrence, relationship or set of experiences as an excusing condition for a patient's current predicament, but if the patient's conduct exceeds all the bounds of excusing (which is why most mental patients *are* mental patients) then we shall still be left with an inexplicable hiatus between such a condition and the patient's state. How far we would wish to go in seeing grounds for excusing and rationalizing an insane person's conduct in something which preceded his admission to mental hospital cannot be settled in advance of any particular instance and certainly not by appeals to 'evidence' or even 'science'. Ultimately, the extent to which we can rationalize someone's insanity depends upon how *charitable* we are prepared to be in assessing background contingencies, and at some point we might be tempted to alter our moral view of a patient entirely in the light of a charitable reading, and begin to construe him as basically sane; but that latter step is a moral step, and there are clearly conventional latitudes of intelligibility that exist which circumscribe our most charitable efforts at redefining someone's psychological status. We are unlikely to carry very many people with us if we venture *too* far (from conventional notions of entitling circumstances for types of action) in relating biographical data to justify any given patient's mode of existence. The two quotations with which I opened this whole chapter illustrate graphically the divergence of moral perspective which underlies the divergence of emphasis in aetiological work; on the one hand, Kallman and Mickey fulminate against sociogenesis, while David Cooper assimilates the problem of schizophrenia to the problem of intrafamilial 'alienation' alone. Neither, I contend, are expressing more than a moral commitment to view the enigma of functional mental disorder in a certain light.

Earlier, in introducing symbolic interactionism, I mentioned two main avenues of research into insanity opened up under that rubric. I have dealt in some detail with the positivistic interactionist work on causation, and I want now to consider the other contribution of interactionist studies which is known variously as 'the societal reaction to deviance' perspective, or, more simply, 'labelling theory'.

Although the labelling theorists do not fully develop a theory encompassing and doing justice to the relationship of insanity to normative order, they are acutely aware of the shortcomings of the 'individual pathology' conception, and stress the role of community members, lay and professional agents of social control and medical/ psychiatric practitioners in 'constructing' a fully-fledged mental patient out of many a reticent psychotic. Edwin Lemert,[53] the pioneer of the societal reaction perspective, writing as long ago as 1951 on these questions from an interactionist viewpoint, suggested that there is a 'surplus of symptoms traceable to the societal reaction'[54] to be found amongst mental patients. What we see as the mental patient's 'insanity' is for Lemert a 'secondary psychotic deviation'[55] superimposed upon primary deviation. In Lemert's terms, primary deviances can be simple and transient violations of cultural expectations, or more gross compulsions, whilst secondary deviances derive from the experience of the reactions of others to primary deviances : 'A person begins to employ his deviant behaviour or a role based on it as a means of defence, attack, or adjustment to the overt and covert problems created by the consequent societal reaction'.[56]

> At each step in the psychotic process there is an interplay between the internal and external limits and the symbolic process [of self-definition], with social failures leading to a distortion of the anticipatory reactions, which attenuate communication and make for more social failures. Because of these failures, subtle or outright rejections and segregational responses of others toward the deviant increase.[57]

This most insightful description of a typical pattern of mutually reinforcing distrust and suspicion heralds a sympathetic but disciplined commonsense discussion of the problem of the self-fulfilling prophecy of labelling deviance. Such a pattern as the one outlined reappears in more detailed form in Lemert's discussion of paranoia. In his paper, 'Paranoia and the Dynamics of Exclusion,'[58] Lemert notes that he does not use as data some 'clinical entity' in the classic Kraepelinian sense'; rather, he concentrates on specifiable dimensions of social processes of exclusion by which a candidate for mental hospitalization is generated and which may be deemed responsible for compounding or reinforcing his paranoid view of the world. Lemert asks if the paranoid's frequently elaborate and consistent reference to a community of responses allegedly loaded against him is a symbolic fabrication of an existentially *real* community. He seeks to conceptualize what he calls paranoid *patterns* in terms of a disorder in communicative reciprocity between the individual and his social milieu, insofar as such patterns assume priority over other activities in social interaction. Addressing himself to Cameron's notion of the 'paranoid pseudo-community,'[59] he remarks that:

> ... while the paranoid person reacts differentially to his social environment, it is also true that 'others' react differentially to him and this reaction commonly if not typically involves covertly organised action and conspiratorial behaviour in a very real sense.[60]

Since these differential reactions are to be understood as reciprocals, it is fair to infer that, for certain persons, discrepant understandings and faulty deductions occurring along a chain of events might lead to some form of social organizational exclusion. Lemert attempts an historical reconstruction of the background processes which culminated in the hospitalization of eight people, and in doing so undertakes exhaustive interviews with all involved; peer groups in place of work, family, police officials and the rest. Concluding, he states certain initiating factors (left largely undescribed, except for instance one case of the loss of a cherished occupational status) and suggests that these led the subjects involved to construe their work mates or office acquaintances in a markedly different light from earlier times. This new treatment was interpreted as odd behaviour by consociates, and a variety of tactics of interpersonal exclusion were said to have begun, closing channels of communication and relationship with the subjects. Under such conditions, a man has :

> ...no means of getting feedback on consequences of his behaviour, which is essential for correcting his interpretations of the social relationships and organisation which he must rely on to define his status and give him identity. He can only read overt behaviour without the informal context.[61]

When contextual particulars are unavailable, and when they seem crucial to the person, he must fall back on (provocative) eliciting strategies such as direct confrontation, and such an activity can be interpreted by consociates (peer group members) as further evidence of strangeness and objectionable social comportment. The processes of exclusion and reinforcement of paranoid patterns can continue through to hospitalization and beyond. Instead of construing the paranoid's ideas of reference to some community of response in terms of Cameron's *'pseudo*-community', Lemert argues that, for some cases at least, it is a real community of response that is being symbolized, not invented.

Lemert's ideas are not devoid of assumptions about the rationality and cognisance of the insane member. He postulates, not a decisive rupture from intelligible social conduct, but a continuing sensitivity towards the opinions, judgments and actions of those around. As I remarked, the impression is given that the initiating factors, or 'primary deviances' in the earlier example, are in themselves of little significance; it is the range of interactional constraints to which the person is subjected which is seen as decisive (perhaps responsible) for his ultimate fate. The individual is deprived of the use of any normalizing techniques; in Lemert's framework, he is not even construed as possessed of any strategic sense or ability to undo wrong impressions. He is at all times a judgemental dope, in

Garfinkel's phrase.[62] And there is no real account of why conspiratorial exclusion, even when socially planned and executed by former friends and colleagues, should result in a symbolic fabrication of such an exclusion (often in the wildest imagery). Lemert tries to stave off any objection that he has not done a strict aetiological study by making reference to his disavowal of Kraepelinian entities as research guiding constructs, but he can only claim, as a result, a very particularistic and impressionistic (albeit wonderfully insightful) 'explanation'. Once again, we find that to read such a study as a decipherment of a mode of insanity, we have to be prepared to accept as comprehensible—even unavoidable—some most peculiar reactions to and constructions upon the conduct of others.

I believe that there have been some misstatements of Lemert's position on social deviance in the work of some of his followers; for example, Howard Becker[63] suggests that we conceive of deviance only as *labelled* deviance, from which it becomes impossible to do justice to ordinary members' distinctions between a member or an activity which *is* deviant (whether overtly or covertly), and a member or an activity which is only *called* deviant. To reformulate Kai Erikson's often cited remark, deviance is not construed *by members* as something conferred upon an act (or a person)—it is construed as a property of that act or person, although of course in making such an identification members are drawing upon their cultural resources as competent judges of such matters. To revert to Becker, it is not that: 'people attach the label "deviant" to others and thereby make deviants of them';[64] on the contrary, if members use such a term in application to someone as the basis for serious inference and further action, they have to be prepared to cite good reasons for so doing, and where they can cite them, the person so labelled is no longer 'merely' labelled, he *is* a bona fide deviant. If we deny the importance of such a distinction, we are doing justice neither to the complexity of members' distinctions nor to the logic of the moral order. Further, deviants can assess themselves as such on the basis of their use of exactly the same logic as other members have at their disposal. If we follow Becker's or Erikson's[65] formulations, we are deprived of the concept of unlabelled deviance, and this is quite basic to social control operations and common judgemental standards (e.g. undetected crime, deviances which 'come to light' only after much probing, etc.). Becker and Erikson conflate primary and secondary deviances and arrive at the conclusion that only the latter exist. In this way, they distort a crucial element in members' ascriptive practices and get into difficulties when pressed to explain the difference, in their terms, between a hard and fast case of criminality or insanity and a case of false arrest, proven innocence or gaslighting. We ordinarily reserve the notion of 'labelling' for the latter, but insist on the objectivity of the former; 'they were, at first, labelled as deviants by the police (the mental health officials) but after the trial (the insanity commission hearing, the psychiatric interview) it became obvious that they *were* in fact deviants'; this seems to be the logic of our moral order, and although we may wish to construe it differently we cannot construe it in any way we like, since the bounds of description, inference and argument are themselves moral bounds (they are invoked when we go too far, produce reasoning that defies our conventions and so on). The morality of social organisation is surely not a topic for arbitrary redefinition by sociologists of all people.

Another mis-statement of labelling theory stems from a recent volume by Spitzer and Denzin, in which they confidently conclude a lengthy exposition on mental patients thus :

> In short, mental illness should be recognised for what it is—a societal reaction to a certain type of behaviour.[66]

Neither Lemert, nor Becker, nor any other labelling theorist has ever proposed that it is the societal reaction itself that is mentally ill; in their terms, the societal reaction constitutes insanity as a *public fact.* Either this statement was simply a slip in expression, or it reveals some quite profound misunderstanding of what is at issue. At best, labelling theory asserts that 'becoming a mental patient is a socially structured event'[67] (or, better, 'process'); at worst, labelling theory degenerates into a quasi-causal theory of insanity in which the societal reaction to some passing rule violation is seen as a determinate variable engendering mental disorder (or the performance of a 'role' of mental disorder) in persons witnessed violating rules. The approach worked out by Thomas Scheff[68] features this latter conception very prominently. For Scheff,

> Entry into a role may be complete when this role is part of the individual's expectations, and when these expectations are reaffirmed in social interaction. In the following pages this principle will be applied to the problem of the causation of mental disorder . . .[69]

In treating insanity as role playing, Scheff is invoking an old sociological metaphor, but it fits rather badly into this field. If we are to take seriously the idea that insane people are literally acting out a role (and in Scheff's analysis, a role built out of the components of learnt stereotypes), then we are left with no genuinely insane people and only a population of frauds. And yet, given the high level of cognisance imputed to the insane by Scheff's theory, this seems to be his unilateral preference. It enables him, for example, to suggest that those who believe quite outrageously bizarre things and attempt to convince others do not *really* hold those beliefs or feel compelled to act in the crazy ways they do; instead, we are urged to think of them as acting uncritically on the basis of a stigmatised role imputed to them by hostile audiences to minor social gaffes.[70] These social gaffes or interpersonal oddities are termed 'residual rule-violations,' and they constitute Scheff's picture of Lemert's 'primary deviance'. They may be 'residual', but they nonetheless (mysteriously) elicit such a shattering soci(et)al reaction that the victim is supposed to internalise without question the audience's imputation of mental derangement. In Scheff's own terms, witnesses' reactions are 'usually the most important determinant of entry' into the 'social role' of madness.[71] At the purely formal level, Scheff's theory could be read as an account of the joker who, on being seen conducting himself in ridiculous ways, in silly antics such as speaking incoherently and the like, is called 'mad' or 'insane' by members of his informal audience, and then takes that as a cue to act the fool some more. This, I believe, quite precisely fits the tenets of Scheff's theory. Since Scheff is dealing with insanity as such, he can hardly allow his theory to encompass anything as trivial as my example and still claim that his is a causal approach to mental disorder. His theory, therefore, is either far too loosely stated, or patently false. It explains on the basis of metaphor, and metaphors which capture phenomena quite distinct from those he addresses.

Scheff faces up to several important issues, however, and despite the failure of his attempt to conceptualize his data adequately, forces us to take stock of some very revealing evidence on screening practices and committal procedures in the United States. He draws attention to the screening of people for insanity in four courts in a midwestern state in the US and reports that such screening is operated on the basis of a wide variety of contingencies, many of which have no relevance (or a remote relevance) to the particular subjects being screened. In approximately a hundred applications for judicial inquiry into mental competency, Scheff reports finding that complainants' testimonies were often brief and garbled. Moreover, the psychiatric examinations were extremely brief and the judges' criteria for incompetency quite extraordinarily vague. He adds:

> The judge, an elected official, runs the risk of being more heavily penalized for erroneously releasing than for erroneously retaining patients. Since the judge personally appoints the panel of psychiatrists to serve as examiners, he can easily transmit the community pressure to them, by failing to reappoint a psychiatrist whose examinations were inconveniently thorough.[72]

Citing Miller's study of fifty-eight committal proceedings, Scheff suggests that many are only 'routine rituals,' with the dice loaded against borderline cases.[73] Kutner's study[74] of committal procedures in parts of the US provides evidence in support of this contention, since psychiatrists appear to arrive at very hasty assessments (frequently after only two or three *minutes*) and then recommend confinement in the great majority of cases on that basis. Scheff concludes that: 'The important decision in hospitalization is that which is made before the complaint comes to court, i.e. in the community and particularly in the family.'[75] There is, however, in Scheff's account, a constant tendency to conceptualize insanity ascriptions as properly the business of professionals; he contrasts the value of a lengthy professional psychiatric interview with the lay ascriptions of family or peer group members in a way which seems to indicate that he thinks the latter likely always to be somehow faulty. In his discussion of the brevity of some of the screening processes and vagueness of the judge's legal criteria for insanity, he occasionally writes as if every single case brought before the psychiatric examiners and the court required long drawn out interviews, even rating scales, and unambiguous legal rules that circumscribed any contingency. Clearly, there will be many cases where insanity is so obviously the only possible verdict that no one's time need be wasted. Furthermore, lacking any 'no decision' options, psychiatrists and judges have to act and as practical men they have neither the time nor the resources for deliberating at inordinate length on borderlines. All practical inquiries have as integral features the properties of making ad hoc decisions on fixed criteria and of making do with whatever it is that is presented as the basis on which a decision must be formulated. (Attention is drawn to Harold Garfinkel's illuminating discussion of the work of the Los Angeles Suicide Prevention Centre with respect to this issue of practical inquiries and their management[16].) This is not meant to excuse the status quo in any way; it is however intended to direct attention away from idealised goals and ideal standards of evaluation and towards the consideration of more specific sorts of objections, of which, no doubt, many can be produced. The question of screening and committal procedures must not be confused with the question of the theoretical claims which Scheff appears to make having considered the evidence on those procedures. He nowhere queries the generality of the assertion that such procedures are ritualistic, nor does he query the very abstract standards by which complainants' testimonies and judges' criteria are found wanting; instead, he takes at face value the results of his own and others' inquiries and erects on their basis an elaborate social control and deviance amplification thesis. In rediscovering what we already knew as practical actors, namely that insanity ascriptions, seriously done as grounds for action, are *not* the exclusive province of specialists, Scheff goes on to present a version of the world within which lay ascriptions are invariably construed as dubious, partisan, truncated or in some other way incompetent. And yet, since cultural competence alone informs one's ability to ascribe, in reasoned and reasonable ways, psychological statuses of all sorts, it is surely peculiar to impute the lack of adequate command over the resources of the culture to all but professional psychiatrists and mental health officials. Any responsible member of a community, with no more than a control over the logic of his moral, social order, can discriminate grossly between insanity and sanity; indeed, given the onus of having to furnish some reasons for an ascription, it is doubtful if that onus does not operate as an important motive for ensuring adequacy of recognition or an effort to assure oneself that one does possess sufficiently convincing evidence, not least to avoid the charge of malice. Sometimes, conspiracies work and innocent people are institutionalized as mentally disordered. But Scheff goes further than this in suggesting that, in the absence of more rigorous screening methods, reliance on community members' ascriptions involves bias against the subject of a competency hearing or hospitalization order. In support of this assumption, he proffers another, which asserts that the contrast between lay and professional ascribers is a contrast between those with no right and those with every right to make ascriptions. This dichotomy does not represent the actual cultural situation from the standpoint of a competent, practical actor, since it is only by virtue of their ability to invoke recognizable cultural resources of judgment that professionals are accorded membership of their specialism *and* ordinary people accorded the status of competent citizen. Cultural competence for any man requires that he should exercise his moral authority whenever and wherever that is deemed appropriate or necessary. Such a prescription underpins the continued cultural support for the practices of professional ratifiers and correcters of lay ascriptions, both in law and psychiatry. Psychiatry, like law but unlike physical medicine, relies exclusively upon the moral authority of the population, however that is mediated, for the conduct of its work. The first court of appeal for professional psychiatry is always the wider cultural standards of judgment operative in society. And such standards are obviously not known and used only by elite sections of society. Indeed, it is precisely the operation of such judgemental resources in the wider community which feeds in subjects for psychiatric (and legal) attention. We should not be surprised that people are capable of making mistakes, acting sometimes from ulterior motives and so forth, but we should, I think, be quite amazed if anyone were to claim that people can *never* be trusted to make psychiatric judgments. After all, lay judgments come first; psychiatric practices differentiate among those judgments, and psychiatric conceptualizations express thought-models which precede and pervade psychiatry itself in that they consist of culturally prepatterned ways of interpreting talk and conduct. If lay judgements are always faulty, then by that criterion psychiatry is in as terrible a predicament itself.

There are several studies that serve to illustrate the contention that people tend to treat insanity ascriptions as very serious concerns, not least because so many of those people who feel required to make such ascriptions are the relatives and kinfolk of those being labelled. Referrals to mental health authorities by family members about one of their number seem to occur some time after the reported 'first instances' of 'bizarre activity'. Intrafamilial processes of accomodation of the deviant member, normalization of interaction and even denials of any problems frequently take place. Rogler and Hollingshead,[77] Jaco,[78] Yarrow and her colleagues,[79] and Sampson and his colleagues[80] have all found that family members report having attentuated any encroaching fears about the faulty psychological status of a co-member, balancing off any 'untoward signs' against other more regular performances on the part of that member, until finally such a pattern of accomodation breaks down. Often, the breakdown takes the form of a 'last straw' incident[81] or critical episode which renders intolerable any continuation of normalizing tactics (which now come to be seen as 'living a lie' or sustaining a pretence). There is no more room for negotiation. There are no remaining excuse clauses. Everything fits retrospectively into place, and the game is up for the member. The public phase of the crisis is ushered in. Of course, this phase does not invariantly take the form of a referral to a psychiatrist or mental health official. Such a referral will depend upon the geographical and ideological availability of psychiatrists and social workers to the referring agent. Other 'help sources' may be preferred.[82]

In the United Kingdom, committal procedures differ from those of the US in important respects, and I shall outline the legal framework a little later on. Most of the theorizing and data discussed in this chapter derive from American experiences.

Sociologists and social psychiatrists, then, approach the enigma of insanity without known organic substratum in diverse ways, but there do seem to be two general directions in which they travel. The first is involved in seeking to infer causal links between elements in a patient's social biography or family history and his current psychiatric status (perhaps seeking to generalize out to a full blown 'theory of schizophrenia'). The second is involved in inquiries into the ways in which social organisation works to allow for the routine processing and management of the mentally disordered. I have tried to demonstrate the insecurity of the former inquiries, based as they must be on treating the psychiatric practitioners' practical operations of diagnosis as unassailable. The suppression or suspension of critical reflection on the problem of sampling and base rates for diagnoses takes its toll in the methodological pitfalls located in the causal studies. Moreover, the use of causal models (or quasi-causal frameworks) for the display of the observations renders equivocal the epistemological basis of the research enterprise as a whole. I want to say a little more about this.

If we read the descriptions of intrafamilial experiences and the rest which are produced by the experiential theorists, we are challenged to see in them adequate grounds for the development of insanity. In other words, we are challenged to evaluate them in terms which would lead us to propose that, had we, or Anyman, been enmeshed in such experiences, then the only option, choice or route left open for us would have been some form of mental disorientation, and a form which would persist. This, I think, is rather an odd challenge. It asks us to presuppose that we know what it is to be driven insane, or even to assume that we could know what insanity means in our own case. That is, it presupposes a solution to the enigma as a prerequisite for adequately evaluating the descriptions. Let us suppose that a former mental patient was given the experiential descriptions to read (or, if they were somewhat technical, then a lengthened and simplified version if that was necessary). Would we expect him to respond to them by saying something like, *that* is the sort of thing which unhinged me, *that* would leave me no option but to become mad (again)? The sense of compulsion, which I assert is missing for the critical reader, would, I believe, also be missing for the former mental patient. If *he* cannot discern a sense of compulsion, then it is very unlikely that sane readers with no background of psychiatric troubles could either. Because of this, no matter how many high correlations are made out between 'social variables' and psychiatric statuses, we still come to feel that something is missing. Either we feel that we lack any adequate statement of how it happens that some people construe the variables in the ways in which the theory asserts that they do, or we tend to believe that those ways, if the theory is correct, constitute no more than firmer evidence of the subjects' ripeness for committal all along. This points up an intractable problem for the would-be experiential decoder of the schizophrenias. His actor model, which gets him from postulated circumstances ABC to postulated reactions XYZ, remains unexplained throughout.

Much of this 'sense of lack' which arises when reading the findings of experiential aetiologists derives from their naïveté about the strength of their observations as vehicles of persuasion. Room for scepticism is always available here due to the faulty logical status of the enterprise in which the descriptions are being developed. A parallel to the correlational approach in this field might be if one read that there was a very high correlation between action X and reason Y; would anyone doubt seriously that action X might be performed quite regularly for a different reason or that reason Y might sensibly and expectably be cited for a different action?

Similarly, one cannot suspend consideration of the possibility that someone could be expected to cope very well in the sort of situations depicted by some of the experiential theorists, whilst others might be thought unable to tolerate a good deal less.

What I have said applies, I think, equally well to the causal theorists within the labelling school. Lemert's patient historical reconstruction essentially consists in the description of a sequence of interactional contingencies which, for some reason left unfathomed, were handled in such a way that the persons so depicted appear to us not only bereft of social skills but quite unable to control their own destinies by means of assertion, denial, manipulation and so on. In other words, the subjects of the reconstructed events seem to have had no choice only if we conceive of them as over-sensitive interpersonal cripples in the first place—and to a degree amounting to a confirmation of their problematic psychological status (paranoia) at the outset, rather than coming to understand the foundations of such a proclivity. I noted earlier that we need to presuppose to a large extent what it is we are having explained to us when we read the bulk of the experiential literature. However, in suggesting that the enigma of functional mental disorders cannot be *solved* that way, I am not advancing the claim that there is some other way in which it can be solved, since I think that it is by virtue of the logical status of the concept of 'insanity' that it must remain an enigma to the rest of us. That is to say, that any attempt to make insanity intelligible is bound to be an attempt to transform that concept, and therefore the nature of what it is that we are trying to render intelligible. When a person's conduct begins to make sense to us, there are no longer inviolable grounds for believing him to be insane; perhaps if we become convinced that such and such is the reason which underpins a man's madness, we should no longer conceive of him as an irrational agent, and maybe we should discharge him from mental hospital or simply deal with him as a socially problematic, in contrast to psychiatrically problematic, person. It makes no sense to claim that a man acts for no apparent reason, can cite no grounds for his conduct, behaves bizarrely and without thought for others, and the like, and then to propose that such insanity reduces to a series of quite rationally and logically related reasons, often of a high intellectual order. Unconventional actions without reasonable grounds most often result in some form of doubt being cast on the actor's psychological status; determining some reasonable grounds ought logically to remove such doubt, at least to the extent of ascribing cognisance and rationality to the actor.

In the next chapter, I want to examine phenomenologically-informed conceptions of insanity and treat the issue of patients' self-reports in some detail, bearing in mind the proceding discussion.

## NOTES

1. F. J. Kallman & J. S. Mickey 'Concept of Induced Insanity in Family Units' *Journal of Nervous and Mental Disorders* vol. 104 (1946)

2. David Cooper *Psychiatry and Anti-Psychiatry* Tavistock Publications (1967) p. 37

3. A. Meyer 'Fundamental Conceptions of Dementia Praecox' *British Medical Journal* No. 2 (1906)

4. L. P. Ullmann & L. Krasner *Case Studies in Behaviour Modification* Holt, Rinehart & Winston (1965)

5. H. J. Eysenck & S. Rachman *The Causes and Cures of Neuroses* London, (1965)

6. E. G. Mishler & N. E. Waxler 'Family Interaction Processes and Schizophrenia: A Review of Current Theories' in G. Handel (ed.) *The Psychosocial Interior of the Family* George Allen & Unwin (1968) pp. 497-8. As a result, of course, the variations in description of 'schizophrenia' are related to the variations in description of family interaction processes produced by the different research teams (p. 497)

7. T. Lidz *et al* 'The Intrafamilial Environment of the Schizophrenic Patient' comprising (1) 'The Father' *Psychiatry, Journal for the Study of Interpersonal Processes* vol. 20 (1957) pp. 329-42 (2) 'Marital Schism and Marital Skew' *American Journal of Psychiatry* vol. 114 (1957) pp. 241-8, (3) 'Parental Personalities and Family Interaction' *American Journal of Orthopsychiatry* vol. 28 (1958) pp. 764-76, (4) 'The Transmission of Irrationality' *Archives of Neurology and Psychiatry* vol. 79 (1958) pp. 305-16 and a book, *The Family and Human Adaptation* Hogarth Press (1964)

8. T. Lidz *et al* 'Marital Schism and Marital Skew', p. 244

9. T. Lidz *The Family and Human Adaptation* op. cit. p. 96

10. On this matter, see E. G. Mishler & N. E. Waxler 'Family Interaction and Schizophrenia: Alternative Frameworks of Interpretation' in D. Rosenthal and S. S. Kety (eds.) *The Transmission of Schizophrenia* Pergamon Press (1968) pp. 213-22 and also Lloyd Rogler 'Does Schizophrenia Disorganise The Family? The Modification of an Hypothesis' in ibid pp. 129-35

11. A sample of such studies would include: W. Brodley 'Some Family

Operations and Schizophrenia' *Archives of General Psychiatry* vol. 1 (1958) pp. 379-402: M. Bowen 'Family Relationships in Schizophrenia' in A. Auerback (ed.) *Schizophrenia: An Integrated Approach* New York, Ronald Press (1959): W. Pollin *et al* 'Family Studies with Twins Discordant for Schizophrenia' *Psychiatry, Journal for the Study of Interpersonal Processes* vol. 28 (1965): Y. O. Alanen 'The Family in the Pathogenesis of Schizophrenia and Neurotic Disorders' *Acta Psychiatrica Scandinavia* vol. 42 No. 189, supplement (1966): L. H. Rogler and A. Hollingshead, *Trapped: Families and Schizophrenia* Wiley (1965): T. Lidz, S. Fleck & A. R. Cornelison *Schizophrenia and the Family* International University Press (1965): J. Haley 'The Family of the Schizophrenic: A Model System' *Journal of Nervous and Mental Disease* vol. 129 (1959) pp. 357-74: J. Haley, 'An Interactional Description of Schizophrenia' *Psychiatry, Journal for the Study of Interpersonal Processes* vol. 22 (1959) pp. 321-32 and D. D. Jackson & J. Weakland 'Schizophrenic Symptoms and Family Interaction' *Archives of General Psychiatry* vol. 1 (1959) pp. 618-21

12.   Manfred Bleuler's recent overview of research on the broken homes hypothesis made reference to widespread inquiries, including the questioning of 3,355 persons, and it concluded that a broken home is on average not more common in the histories of diagnosed schizophrenics than in the population as a whole ('Some Results of Research in Schizophrenia' *Behavioural Science* vol. 15 No. 3 (1970) p. 215). Clearly, a home can be 'broken' in a wide variety of ways (e.g. one spouse dying, deserting, being imprisoned or divorced, etc), and no breakdown along these dimensions was mentioned.

13.   Herbert Blumer 'Sociological Analysis and the "Variable" in J. G. Manis & B. N. Meltzer (eds) *Symbolic Interaction* Allyn & Bacon (1967) pp. 84-94

14.   ibid p. 91

15.   ibid p. 93; Blumer notes that most of the categories deployed as variables in social research are polymorphous, lacking fixed or uniform indicators 'Irrespective of how one may subsequently combine a number of [variables]—in an additive manner, a clustering, a chain-like arrangement, or a "feedback" scheme—the objective of variable research is initially to isolate a simple and fixed relation between two variables. For this to be done each of the two variables must be set up as a distinct item with a unitary qualitative make-up.' (p. 91)

16.   A. B. Hollingshead & F. C. Redlich *Social Class and Mental Illness* New York, John Wiley & Sons (1958)

17.   R. Faris & H. W. Dunham *Mental Disorders in Urban Areas* New York, Hafner (1960)

18.   Leo Srole *et al Mental Health in the Metropolis* vols. 1 & 2 New York McGraw-Hill (1962)

19.   B. Pasamanick (ed.) *Epidemiology of Mental Disorder* Washington DC, American Association for the Advancement of Science (1959)

20.   J. A. Clausen & M. L. Kohn 'The Ecological Approach in Social Psychiatry' *American Journal of Sociology* vol. 40 (1954) pp. 140-49

21.  H. W. Dunham 'Social Structures and Mental Disorders: Competing Hypotheses of Explanation' in *Causes of Mental Disorders: A Review of Epidemiological Knowledge* New York, Millbank Memorial Fund, (1961) p. 230; cited in Alex Robertson 'Sociology and the Study of Psychiatric Disorder' *The Sociological Review* vol. 17 No. 3 (1969) p. 382

22.  Alex Robertson, ibid p. 384

23.  Leo Srole *et al,* op. cit. (note 18 above)

24.  L. C. Wynne, I. Ryckoff, J. Day & S. Hirsch 'Pseudo-mutuality in the Family Relations of Schizophrenics' *Psychiatry, Journal for the Study of Interpersonal Processes* vol. 21 (1958) pp. 205-20

25.  ibid p. 213

26.  ibid p. 205

27.  G. Bateson, D. D. Jackson, J. Haley & J. Weakland 'Toward a Theory of Schizophrenia' *Behavioural Science* vol. 1 (1956) pp. 251-64

28.  This was further confirmed in personal communication cited by Mishler & Waxler, 'Family Interaction Processes and Schizophrenia: A Review . . . ,' op. cit. p. 478

29.  B. Schuham 'The Double-Bind Hypothesis a Decade Later' *Psychological Bulletin* vol. 6 (December 1967)

30.  ibid

31.  J. Weakland, 'The Double-Bind Hypothesis of Schizophrenia and Three-Party Interaction' in D. D. Jackson (ed.) *The Aetiology of Schizophrenia* New York, Basic Books (1960) pp. 373-88

32.  P. Watzlawick 'A Review of the Double-Blind Theory' *Family Process* vol. 2 (1963) pp. 132-53. For a study influenced by double-bind theory yet differing from it in important respects, see Yi-Chuang Lu 'Contradictory Parental Expectations in Schizophrenia' *Archives of General Psychiatry* vol. 6 (1962) pp. 219-34

33.  E. G. Mishler & N. E. Waxler 'Family Interaction Processes and Schizophrenia: A Review . . .' op. cit., p. 512

34.  H. Blumer 'Social Psychology' in E. P. Schmidt (ed.) *Man and Society* Prentice-Hall (1937). See also Blumer's collection of papers in his *Symbolic Interactionism: Perspective and Method* Prentice-Hall (1969)

35.  Manford H. Kuhn 'Major Trends in Symbolic Interaction Theory in the Past Twenty-Five Years' in J. G. Manis & B. N. Meltzer (eds.) *Symbolic Interaction* Boston, Allyn & Bacon (1967) p. 49

36.  J. Gibson 'The Concept of Stimulus' *The American Psychologist* vol. 15 (1960) pp. 694-703

37.  Noam Chomsky 'Review of "Verbal Behaviour" by B. F. Skinner New York, Appleton-Century-Crofts (1957)' *Language* vol. 35 (1959) pp. 26-58. See also H. G. Burger's comments on J. A. Jones 'Operant Psychology and the Study of Culture' *Current Anthropology* vol. 12 No. 2 (April 1971) pp. 179-80

38.  Manford H. Kuhn & Thomas S. McPartland 'An Empirical Investigation of Self-Attitudes' *American Sociological Review* vol. 19 (1954) pp. 68-76

39.  This problem of the divergence between some abstract measure and any set of engaged activities is characteristic also of the intelligence

quotient tests. Herbert Blumer, in a long attack on operationalism in sociology and social psychology, wrote: '. . . Intelligence is seen in empirical life as present in such varied things as the skilful military planning of an army general, the ingenious exploitation of a market situation by a business entrepreneur, effective methods of survival by a disadvantaged slum dweller, the clever meeting of the problems of his world by a peasant or a primitive tribesman, the cunning of low-grade delinquent girl morons in a detention home, and the construction of telling verse by a poet. It should be immediately clear how ridiculous and unwarranted it is to believe that the operationalising of intelligence through a given intelligence test yields a satisfactory picture of intelligence.' (H. Blumer *Symbolic Interactionism* op. cit. p. 31: section on methodology). This does not gainsay the practical utility of such measures; but it does suggest their limits when used as underpinnings for theory construction.

40.   T. S. McPartland & J. H. Cumming 'Self-Conception, Social Class and Mental Health' *Human Organisation* vol. 17 No. 33 (1958) pp. 24-9

41.   T. S. McPartland, J. H. Cumming & W. S. Garretson 'Self-Conception and Ward Behaviour in Two Psychiatric Hospitals' in J. G. Manis & B. N. Meltzer (eds.) *Symbolic Interaction* op. cit. pp. 445-58

42.   The citation is from R. Taylor, *Action and Purpose* Prentice-Hall (1966) p. 138. The works of and about George Herbert Mead used as the resource for discussing his philosophy of self and action are as follows: *Mind, Self and Society* ed. C. W. Morris, Phoenix Edition, University of Chicago Press (1967); Anselm Strauss (ed.), *George Herbert Mead on Social Psychology* University of Chicago Press (1964); B. N. Meltzer, *The Social Psychology of George Herbert Mead* Centre for Sociological Research, Western Michigan University (1964) and Maurice Natanson *The Social Dynamics of George H. Mead* Washington D.C., Public Affairs Press (1956).

43.   R. Taylor *Action and Purpose* op. cit. p. 136

44.   Ernest Becker 'Mills' Social Psychology and the Great Historical Convergence on the Problem of Alienation' in I. L. Horowitz (ed.) *The New Sociology* Oxford University Press (1965) esp. pp. 122-29

45.   ibid, p. 125. See also the extended discussion of these questions in Becker's book, *The Revolution in Psychiatry: The New Understanding of Man* New York (1964).

46.   G. A. Kelly *The Psychology of Personal Constructs, Vols. 1 & 2* New York, Norton Press (1955). Bannister provides a useful though schematic exegesis of Kelly's approach in his article 'A New Theory of Personality' in Brian Foss (ed.) *New Horizons in Psychology* Pelican (1966) pp. 361-80 and his specifically psychiatrically-based usage of Kelly's perspective appears in his 'The Nature and Measurement of Schizophrenic Thought-Disorder' *Journal of Mental Science* vol. 108 (1962) pp. 825-30 and in later papers.

47.   D. Bannister 'The Genesis of Schizophrenic Thought-Disorder: Retest of the Serial Invalidation Hypothesis' *British Journal of Psychiatry* vol. 111 (1965) pp. 377-81

48.   D. Bannister & P. Salmon 'Schizophrenic Thought-Disorder:

Specific or Diffuse?' *British Journal of Medical Psychology,* Vol. 39 (1966), p. 217. See also F. M. McPherson & F. Buckley 'Thought-Process Disorder and Personal Construct Subsystems' *British Journal of Social and Clinical Psychology* vol. 9 (1970) pp. 380-1. It ought to be noted that Bannister and Salmon base their clinical depictions on observations of eleven subjects 'unanimously judged by consultant, registrar and psychologist to manifest in interview the clinical characteristic of thought disorder—blocking, irrelevance, poverty of content, etc.' (op. cit.) A lineup of authoritative figures is, I suppose, provided to give us confidence or trust in the identification of 'the phenomenon'.

49. T. Lidz, A. Cornelison, D. T. Carlson & S. Fleck, 'Intrafamilial Environment of the Schizophrenic Patient: The Transmission of Irrationality' *Archives of Neurology and Psychiatry* vol. 79 No. 3 (1958) p. 306

50. Stephen Fleck 'Family Dynamics and Origin of Schizophrenia' in Ohmer Milton & Robert G. Wahler (eds). *Behaviour Disorders. Perspectives and Trends* 2nd Edition, J. B. Lippincott Co. (1969) p. 111 et seq

51. ibid

52. D. Bannister & P. Salmon op. cit. p. 219

53. E. M. Lemert *Social Pathology* McGraw-Hill (1951)

54. ibid pp. 442-43. This idea strikes one at first as convincing, but troubles arise, as one is left stranded when one seeks something like a 'norm' for symptom presentations by which to assess a 'surplus', and the notion of such a surplus being 'traceable to' societal reaction(s) comes to appear quite vague. Perhaps the best that could be made of this assertion is to suppose that people who are mentally disordered encounter strained interpersonal relationships which leave little room for anything but conduct which itself is strained and easily assimilable by witnesses into 'the patient's condition,' rather than attributable to interactional difficulties created out of a recognition of the imbalanced role relationships (sane/insane, patient/lay observer, etc).

55. ibid p. 428

56. ibid p. 76 (italicised in original text)

57. ibid p. 428

58. E. M. Lemert 'Paranoia and the Dynamics of Exclusion' in Earl Rubington & Martin S. Weinberg (eds.) *Deviance: The Interactionist Perspective* Macmillan (1968) pp. 99-108. The article was first published in 1962.

59. Norman Cameron 'The Paranoid Pseudo-Community Revisited' *American Journal of Sociology* vol. 65 (1959) pp. 52-8

60. E. M. Lemert op. cit. (1968) p. 100

61. ibid, p. 107

62. Harold Garfinkel *Studies in Ethnomethodology* Prentice-Hall (1967) pp. 66-8. Garfinkel uses this notion to deal with the fact that theorists in the non-biological human sciences need to postulate actor models with specific (though often unspecified) features if their inferences are to be constructed intelligibly and consistently from the use of variable analytic procedures. Garfinkel is *not* suggesting that sociologists and

psychologists are positing stupid homunculi; the point is that whatever models of the actor *are* implicit, they must be bereft of the commonsense rationalities of judgement over courses of action in order that what is reported as having occurred can be construed as having occurred as the result of following certain *necessary* and/or *invariant* pathways. The actor model's judgmental operations are conceived as isomorphic with those of the investigator who must needs deprive his data of perspectival choice etc.

63. H. S. Becker, *Outsiders: Studies in the Sociology of Deviance* Glencoe, Free Press (1963); on p. 9, Becker remarks that: 'deviance is not a quality of the act the person commits, but rather a consequence of the application by others of rules and sanctions to an "offender". The deviant is one to whom that label has successfully been applied; deviant behaviour is behaviour that people so label.'

64. H. S. Becker 'Introduction' to his edited anthology *The Other Side: Perspectives on Deviance* Glencoe, Free Press (1964) p. 3. The entire approach displayed by Becker here and elsewhere seems to stem from the dissatisfaction with orthodox criminology and deviancy theory that colludes with official social control agents in 'identifying' deviance and then furnishing causal models for it. Whilst it may very well be true that we have no further *explanations* of any weight or substance for deviances other than those provided by deviants themselves or their ideological rationalisers and opponents, it is nonetheless the case that deviance in any form is more than simply a matter of powerful people invoking a label and applying it to people. That 'more' may not be a constant biological or psychological propensity—rather, it seems to involve complex judgemental work in its identification, the logic of which would seem more interesting and fruitful to study than 'the phenomenon' or 'its causes'. For a start in this direction, see Aaron V. Cicourel *The Social Organisation of Juvenile Justice* John Wiley & Sons (1968), and, for a more technical discussion, Melvin Pollner 'On the Foundations of Mundane Reasoning' unpublished PhD thesis, University of California, June 1970, especially pp. 173 et seq and pp. 72-101.

65. Kai T. Erikson 'Notes on the Sociology of Deviance' in H. S. Becker (ed.) *The Other Side . . .*, op. cit.; in Erikson's terms, 'Deviance is not a property *inherent in* certain forms of behaviour; it is a property *conferred upon* these forms by the audiences which directly or indirectly witness them.' (p. 11) Cf. the citation from Becker above (note 63).

66. Stephan P. Spitzer & Norman K. Denzin, *The Mental Patient: Studies in the Sociology of Deviance* New York, McGraw-Hill (1968) p. 464

67. Harold Sampson, Sheldon L. Messinger & Robert D. Towne 'Family Processes and Becoming a Mental Patient' *American Journal of Sociology* vol. 68 (1962) p. 88

68. Thomas J. Scheff *Being Mentally Ill: A Sociological Theory* Weidenfeld & Nicolson (1966).

69. ibid pp. 63-4

70. ibid Chapter Two, 'Residual Deviance' (pp. 31-54)

71.   ibid p. 28

72.   T. J. Scheff (with David M. Culver) 'Legal and Psychiatric Screening of Incoming Patients' in T. J. Scheff, *Being Mentally Ill . . .* op. cit. p. 153

73.   D. Miller 'County Lunacy Commission Hearings: Some Observations of Commitment to a State Mental Hospital' *Social Problems* (cited in Scheff, ibid, p. 133). Mishler & Waxler's work on the Massachusetts Mental Health Centre concluded that as many as 39% of applications did not result in hospitalization. (E. G. Mishler & N. E. Waxler 'Decision Processes in Psychiatric Hospitalization; Patients Referred, Accepted, and Admitted to a Psychiatric Hospital' *American Sociological Review* vol. 28 (1963) pp. 576-87

74.   Luis Kutner 'The Illusion of Due Process in Commitment Proceedings' in T. J. Scheff (ed.), *Mental Illness and Social Processes* Harper & Row (1967) pp. 102-08

75.   Thomas J. Scheff 'Social Conditions for Rationality: How Urban and Rural Courts Deal with the Mentally Ill' in his book (op. cit.) and as a paper in his edited collection, *Mental Illness and Social Processes* op. cit. p. 117

76.   Harold Garfinkel 'Practical Sociological Reasoning: Some Features in the Work of the Los Angeles Suicide Prevention Center' in Edwin S. Schneidman (ed.) *Essays in Self-Destruction* International Science Press (1967) and as partially reproduced in 'Practical Sociological Reasoning: Doing Accounts in "Common Sense Situations of Choice" ' *Studies in Ethnomethodology* Englewood Cliffs, N.J. (Prentice-Hall, 1967) pp. 11-18

77.   L. H. Rogler & A. Hollingshead *Trapped: Families and Schizophrenia* New York, Wiley (1965)

78.   G. Jaco *The Social Epidemiology of Mental Disorders* New York, Russell Sage Foundation (1960)

79.   M. R. Yarrow, C. G. Schwartz, H. S. Murphy & L. C. Deasy 'The Psychological Meaning of Mental Illness in the Family' in E. Rubington & M. S. Weinberg (eds.) *Deviance: The Interactionist Perspective* op. cit. pp. 31-41

80.   H. Sampson *et al* op. cit.

81.   Kathleen Smith, Murial W. Pumphrey and Julian C. Hall 'The "Last Straw"; Decision Incidents Resulting in the Request for Hospitalization in One Hundred Schizophrenic Patients' *American Journal of Psychiatry* vol. 120 (1963) pp. 228-33. See also Carroll A. Whitmer & Glenn C. Conover, 'A Study of Critical Incidents in the Hospitalization of the Mentally Ill' *Social Work* vol. 4 (January 1959) pp. 89-94. For a detailed account of US committal procedures, consult S. Kirson Weinberg 'The Commitment of Patients to the Mental Hospital' in his edited anthology *The Sociology of Mental Disorders: Analyses and Readings in Psychiatric Sociology* Staples Press (1968) pp. 182-3. A similar formal account can be found in Albert Deutsch, *The Mentally Ill in America* New York, Columbia University Press, (1949) p. 428 . . .

82.   D. L. Phillips 'Rejection: A Possible Consequence of Seeking Help

for Mental Disorders' *American Sociological Review* vol. 28 (1963) pp. 963-72. Phillips considers clergymen and physicians as common help sources outside formal, medical psychiatric facilities and psychiatric social work agents.

# CHAPTER THREE

# Phenomenological Conceptions of Schizophrenia

Clinicians who have sought to theorize about their practical involvement with psychiatrically disturbed individuals have often found
an amenable framework for the organisation of their observations
in a theoretical tradition called 'phenomenology'. I cannot
characterise phenomenology very succinctly, since its breadth and
complexity defy both definitive listing of 'central tenets' and
schematic summaries, and for our purposes an attempt at a general
exposition would be too long a digression. However, at the risk of
oversimplifying things, I must provide something of a background
for the ideas I want to treat in this section, and of necessity that
requirement will take us into the territory of phenomenological
philosophy.

Perhaps it is best to let some of the most influential philosophers
in this tradition speak for themselves. Edmund Husserl, the
founder of what Spiegelberg terms the 'phenomenological move-
ment,' writing in the early part of this century, conducted a series
of investigations into what he termed 'the crisis of the European
sciences,' charging them, amongst other things, with seeking to
'naturalize' the phenomena of experience.[1] The atomistic and
associationist psychologies of Hume and Mill, and the burgeoning
of an experimental science of psychology, were considered by
Husserl and his followers to represent variations of an attempt to :

> ... reduce all mental operations, attitudes and states to sensations
> and their echoes, randomly coagulated by association, inevitably
> [eliminating] just what make the differences between thinking
> and mere wandering, between choice and mere impulse, between
> judgement and mere fancy, between inference and mere
> suggestion, between doubt and mere vacancy[2]

Gilbert Ryle, whose words these are, demonstrated (in a vastly under-valued paper on phenomenology[3]) how Husserl reacted against elementaristic views on perception and mental functioning by postulating an overall integrative conception he entitled 'the intentionality of consciousness'. Husserl wrote :

> ... *every* intentional experience—and this is indeed the fundamental mark of all intentionality—has its "intentional object," i.e.; its objective meaning. Or to repeat the same in other words : to have a meaning, or to have something 'in mind,' is the cardinal feature of all consciousness.[4]

From here, Husserl took it that, since all consciousness is 'consciousness *of*' something, the link between the human subject and the world is *intrinsic*. Moreover, the doctrine of intentionality specified that to every case of mental functioning of whatever sort there must be a correlative 'intentional object'. Husserl took it that knowing, believing, desiring and judging (for example) were mental operations with intentional objects—he thought it possible to construe many diverse forms of mental functioning under the overall rubric of 'intentionality'. For this, he had to propose that we have on the one hand 'acts of consciousness' (believing, judging, desiring etc) and on the other hand the 'objects or contents' of these 'acts'. However, as Ryle remarked, believing, desiring, knowing and many other 'mental' terms do not denote 'acts' at all, even though they are expressible in active verbs. We can say of someone that he knew, believed or desired something for several months or years, but we could not say of him that at any particular moment he was engaged in or occupied with knowing, believing or desiring.[5] In Husserl's scheme, phenomenological analysis was designed to fathom the 'essences' of the acts and objects of consciousness; rather than systematically unpacking the disparities between mental concepts in human discourse, phenomenologists were to engage in the disciplined reflection upon their own streams of experience (the process of 'phenomenological reduction' in which mundane presuppositions about the world were, as far as possible, to be bracketed). In so doing, they were conducting a 'scientific' investigation which was supposed to be a priori and yet underpin the empirical, natural sciences with an essential core of absolute truths about the experienced world. Phenomenology was conceived in this sense as a kind of 'super-science', with its own realm of facts and its own method. Nowhere are we given unobjectionable analyses which reveal to us the 'essences' of believing or desiring, and this is perhaps because those categories are polymorphous and resist distillation into 'essentialist' terms. In fact, the products of the 'eidetic' (essentialist) reduction are largely poetic redescriptions of mundane objects or artfully constructed intuitions about variations in perception (often conflated with 'experience').

Phenomenology became an important intellectual weapon in the armoury of philosophers involved in the critique of psychological and sociological determinisms. Merleau-Ponty's remarks on the phenomenological project make this quite clear :

> I am not the outcome or the meeting point of numerous causal agencies which determine my bodily or psychological make-up. I cannot conceive myself as nothing but a bit of the world, a mere object of biological, psychological or sociological investigation. I cannot shut myself up in the realm of science. All my knowledge of the world, even my scientific knowledge, is gained from my own particular point of view, or from some experience of the world without which the symbols of science would be meaningless. The whole universe of science is built upon the world as directly experienced . . . .[6]

Merleau-Ponty considers consciousness to be a 'realm' of absolutely unique priority since it reveals itself as the medium of access to whatever exists. Thus, as Gurvitch writes :

> . . . aiming at ultimate clarification and justification of all knowledge and experience, phenomenology considers acts of consciousness primarily, if not exclusively, with regard to their cognitive or presentational function . . . . phenomenological investigations must be carried out in a *strictly* descriptive orientation.[7]

In seeking to 'return' to the data of experience *(Erlebnisse)*, phenomenologists seem to assume a disjunction between *all* events and our experiences of them, as if there is always an intrinsic difference between my description of a thing or event and my description of my conscious experience of a thing or event. They do a great service when they remind us that scientific knowledge (like all shared knowledge) has an *intersubjective* character, and not an objectivistic independence of a community of experiencing inquirers; but they confuse us when they appear to assert that there is a 'phenomenal world' or a 'phenomenal field' somehow superimposed over, or co-occurrent with, the external world.[8] In terms of its general onslaught against determinism and elementarism in the study of human action and perception, phenomenology insists upon the primacy of the 'experiential structuring' of the sensory field. By this I understand something like the following. Katz, as long ago as 1911, published a work[9] in which he insisted that we begin with the phenomena of colour experience rather than with stimuli or sensation elements (such as the impact of millimicrons of wave-length on specialised sensory receptors). Katz showed that the same colour (by wavelength or spectrum reading) can be perceived as lustrous, filmy or shadowed on a surface depending upon the mode of presentation; as MacLeod put it :

> The surface appearance is not a simple function of the wave length or intensity of incoming light; it is a complex function of many variables which contribute to the structuring of the visual world.[10]

Merleau-Ponty's discussion of the Müller-Lyer experience in his *The Structure of Behaviour*[11] is also addressed to the problem of elementarism. The Müller-Lyer figure is composed of two prallel lines of the same measurable length placed on a flat ground with one of the lines capped each end with arrow-heads and the other with wing-like extensions. Merleau-Ponty accounts for our regular perceptual judgment that the wing-capped line is longer than the other by suggesting that the line with arrowheads represents the 'experience of closure' whilst the line with wings represents the 'experience of extension'.

Both the Katz and the Müller-Lyer phenomena present us with data that cannot fit into an elementaristic account, although both have received quite convincing alternative interpretations other than phenomenological ones. The observation that certain facts about perception cannot be reduced without residue to explanations in terms of the properties of stimuli and the physiological organs for processing them does not imply that we are dealing with a separate realm of existence—'the phenomenal field'—which forms a discrete area for investigation. Indeed, I believe that most if not all of the analyses of sensation and perception adduced by pheno-menologists which make reference to such a field or 'world' can be adequately recast in terms of a 'contextual' or environmental-relativistic framework. In this sense, the famous experiment con-ducted by Bruner[12] which found differential judgments on the size of ordinary American coins amongst poor and rich children (the poorer children 'seeing' the coins as larger than the rich ones) can be given a contextualist interpretation without any loss of sense or explanatory adequacy. There is no need to invoke the vocabulary of 'differential phenomenal worlds' and so on.

In psychopathology, thinkers such as Karl Jaspers distinguished between the substance of Husserl's programme for a 'descriptive psychology' of human experience and the practice of seeking out the 'essences' of noetic acts (acts of consciousness), and in so doing laid the foundations for phenomenological studies of insanity, especially schizophrenia.

Phenomenological influences on psychopathology and psychoanalytic theory were restricted to European thinkers such as Binswanger, Sartre, Jaspers and Minkowski until a handful of American and British psychiatric researchers began making use of phenomenological ideas after the Second World War. Descriptive psychology, embellished with phenomenological terminology, focussing upon patients' own reports of their experiences of mental disorder, became a favoured alternative to the various forms of aetiological work being done within a positivistic tradition in psychopathology. In a recently published paper of 1912[13] Jaspers noted that no attempts were made to deal with causation (aetiology) by phenomenologically-oriented psychopathologists, and in his celebrated text *General Psychopathology*[14] he remarked that it is not so much the number of cases seen that matters in phenomenological research, 'but the extent of the inner exploration of the individual case, which needs to be carried to the furthest possible limit'.[15] Patients' self-descriptions are presented, described, differentiated and explored; the prejudgment of psychiatric disorder is not allowed to invalidate the possible sense to be determined in their communications, and analysis aims at uncovering comprehensible, rational relationships between the elements of patients' accounts of their experiences.

> Theoretically we talk of incoherence, dissociation, fragmenting of consciousness, intrapsychic ataxia, weakness of apperception, insufficiency of psychic activity and disturbance of association etc . . . . We call the behaviour crazy or silly but all these words simply imply in the end that there is a common element of the "ununderstandable". '[16]

Phenomenological description is carried out with the aim of interpreting, rendering intelligible, the reported experiences of mental patients, and so the primary requirement here (as with all attempts at *epoché,* or the suspension of mundane presuppositions as far as possible) is that what the particular patient says shall not be considered as either the coerced emissions of a faulty brain and nervous system or as the products of irrational training in language, culture and morality. R. D. Laing, one of the most influential of the phenomenologically inspired writers on schizophrenia, suggests that we view the 'psychotic' as a person labelled on the grounds that there has been some disjunction in his relationships with the labeller ('It is only because of this interpersonal disjunction,' he continues, 'that we start to examine his urine, and look for anomalies in the graphs of the electrical activity of his brain.')[17] In dealing with the self-descriptions and experiential accounts of the psychotic, Laing proposes that we are simply confronted with a problem in hermeneutics; although he does note that in certain respects the problem in this field has aspects lacking in others :

> The difficulties facing us here are somewhat analogous to the difficulties facing the expositor of hieroglyphics, an analogy Freud was fond of drawing; they are, if anything, greater. The theory of the interpretation or deciphering of hieroglyphics and other ancient texts has been carried further forward and made more explicit by Dilthey in the last century than the theory of the interpretation of psychotic 'hieroglyphic' speech and actions.[18]

Laing goes on to suggest that formal, clinical schemes of classification of mental disorders resemble the formal analysis of documents in terms of syntax and stylistic structure, wherein typological concerns overshadow interpretive ones. In terms of the hermeneutical issue, Laing draws attention to the different foundations informing Dilthey's theory of interpretation and phenomenological interpretations of psychotic communications respectively. In the former, the assumption is that the expositor does not stand in an entirely different context of lived experience from the author of the text. That is, he must share sufficient of the beliefs and categories of the author and his period to enable him to sustain translation hypotheses. There must be *some* constants in the structuring of experience (conceptual frameworks) and thence in 'ontological commitments'; without these, no interpretation can be anchored, and no selection between competing translations can be facilitated. In the latter case (interpretations of psychotic communication), little or no communality of reference can be found in so many cases reported in clinical texts. Indeed, there are quite often decisive linguistic and ontologically defined barriers between patient and analyst. For example, unless some regularities can be discerned in the communicative outpourings of the diagnosed schizophrenic, then he (the 'schizophrenic') cannot even be said to be using a code. Unless there is some kind of code, there is no logical possibility of cracking it! With regard to the 'ontologically-defined' barriers between the patient and his would-be interpreter, I make reference to the articulation by some patients of beliefs or self-conceptions that make themselves out to be other than human (e.g. corpses, machines, robots etc), and which inform a completely closed system of thinking. I shall return to this problem later.

It is useful to contrast the in-depth hermeneutical exercise of phenomenological analysis with the standard psychiatric interview. The psychiatric interview typically includes the questioning of patients to 'reveal' any 'signs and symptoms' that may be subdued or temporarily absent. The elicitation of 'thought disorder' by means of requesting the patient to complete a supposedly well known proverbial expression is a classical example. Asking the date is another tactic, this time for revealing evidence of disorientation. Now it seems clear that psychiatric interviews are generally structured by the exigencies of time and resources, and rarely have as their aim the deepening of the understanding of the patient. In fact, somatic techniques are most often deployed in cases of psychosis in the United Kingdom, since few practical clinicians have either the theoretical inclination or the resources for sustained psychotherapy and depth analysis of highly mentally-disordered persons. Psychiatric interviews, then, may fairly be claimed to be ad hoc and wholly practical encounters. On the other hand, phenomenological analysis of the self-reported experiences of mental patients appears to take place with a select few. A good deal of pre-selection of cases (by GPs, mental health social workers and hospital officials) takes place whereby the phenomenologically oriented clinician is presented with a filtered group of persons thought best suited to his particular orientation. Sometimes, the clinician himself selects a sample of patients for depth-analytic work. This, I think, helps us to put two things in perspective. First, it might clarify the basis of those claims made by psychiatric readers of Laing's own work and the work of other phenomenologists that their patients are neither 'true' nor 'representative' schizophrenics or psychotics. They seem, runs the argument, more intellectually able, more reflective, more garrulous, articulate and insightful than the common run of psychotic patients. (Hugo Meynell's recent paper on Laing,[19] one of the few discussions of Laing to treat the central issues rigorously, takes up this issue in further detail). Secondly, we are in a better position to understand the quite radical disjunction between phenomenologically-oriented encounters and standard psychiatric interviews. The former are addressed to the revelation of patients' experiences in as unstructured a manner as possible, without, as we have noted, any inhibiting presupposition of causal mechanisms or disease processes underlying the patients' accounts. The latter are addressed to the practical exigencies of determining the extent of the patient's disorder, with an eye to the appropriateness of some ward and treatment schedule. There, 'psychotic' means something like inability to function and in need of specialized medical care and custodial attention, whilst in the former encounters, 'psychotic' means, as we have seen from Laing's remarks, something like 'label bestowed due to disjunction in social relationships'—hardly useful as grounds for further therapeutic inference and action.

Given these divergences in the auspices governing the two encounters, it seems a little strange to use one as the means of belittling the other (i.e. to construe the psychiatric interviews which occur in busy mental hospitals as poor versions of phenomenological encounters). However, Laing is interested in beginning an overall moral argument about psychiatry as practised. He begins his critique with some remarks on how his own patients seem to him to differ from psychiatric stereotypes :

> ... except in the case of chronic schizophrenics, I have difficulty in actually discovering the "signs and symptoms" of psychosis in persons I am myself interviewing.[20]

and he goes on to speculate that the reason for this might be that :

> The standard psychiatric texts contain the descriptions of the behaviour of people in a behavioural field that includes the psychiatrist. The behaviour of the patient is to some extent a function of the behaviour of the psychiatrist in the same behavioural field. The standard psychiatric patient is a function of the standard psychiatrist, and of the standard mental hospital.[21]

The 'typical' or standard patient for the Tavistock existential phenomenologist does seem quite likely to differ from the typical patient for the somatotherapist in a large Northern mental hospital, but this is open to various explanations, and should not lead us to infer that the conduct of a patient is a 'function' of his psychiatrist or institution as if the behavioural field (by which I take it Laing means the field of interaction) were a determinant of uniformity or conformity. Even if we accept that total institutions such as mental hospitals regulate conduct with a morass of instructions and a tightly-spun web of rules, we are not obliged to presume that a patient's delusions and hallucinations are subtle responses to his interactional dealings with his therapist and therefore we are witnessing a normal person constrained into such abnormalities by virtue of psychiatric regimes. It would be hard to persuade a somatotherapist that his patient, whom (let us say) he describes to us as 'out of touch with reality' is, in fact, the partial product of the communicative work of therapist and patient! If we *did* sustain such a claim, the somato-therapist would be a likely candidate for institutionalization himself, perhaps on the grounds of *folie à deux*.

Laing's thesis develops from the following perspective:

> Some people labelled schizophrenic (not all, and not necessarily) manifest behaviour in words, gestures, actions (linguistically, paralinguistically and kinetically) that is unusual. Sometimes (not always and not necessarily) this unusual behaviour (manifested to us, the others, as I have said, by sight and sound) expresses, wittingly or unwittingly, unusual experiences that the person is undergoing. Sometimes (not always and not necessarily) these unusual experiences that are expressed by unusual behaviour appear to be part of a potentially orderly, natural sequence of experiences.[22]

These remarks are at once cautious and chimerical. A handful, at least, of those persons labelled 'psychotic' or 'schizophrenic', are thought to be involved in existential voyages to the inner world of psychic space, voyages which men have been making since antiquity but which, in our own state of capture we call civilization, we can only recognise as illness. These ideas derive from (or perhaps are tried out on) clinical experiences with certain patients. Laing presents a transcription, with accompanying interpretive commentary, of a subject's recollections of a psychotic 'episode' (a voyage 'into inner space and time') recorded twenty-four years afterwards.[23] A feature of this voyaging is 'ego-loss', wherein a danger is that: 'One's own ego-less mind may be confused with one's ego.'[24] A profusion of similarly metaphoric and apocalyptic imagery follows; the narrative is suffused with poetry and rhetoric. In whatever way the subject has come to be precipitated on such a 'voyage', it is not the voyage itself which he needs to be cured of, since this is taken to be : 'a natural way of healing our own appalling state of alienation called normality'.[25]

The patient's self-description is allowed to generate a wild, imaginative commentary oscillating between metaphoric description ('the self wishes to be wedded to and embedded in the body, yet is constantly afraid to lodge in the body . . .'[26]) and ordinary-language hermeneutics ('Jesse felt that he had enhanced powers of control over his body and could affect others'[27]). Laing treats his subject's utterances both as resources for the exemplification of theoretical notions ('ontological insecurity' and 'self body split'), some of which he borrows from Sartre, some from Heidegger, and also as sketchy accounts in need of repair from time to time. We switch from a specialised sublanguage, probably quite foreign to the interlocutor, to paraphrasing and fillers-in with terms that do not significantly depart from the overall manner in which the subject is himself speaking. When Laing engages in the use of his sublanguage, we are supposed to see in that an attempt at illumination or clarification; but it is here where we cannot be sure who is the better authority—analyst or analysand. Since his subject is cited as speaking coherent, albeit poetic, English sentences, it seems a little odd to see Laing as decoding them in a manner analogous to the translation of an alien tongue. Furthermore, translating an alien tongue presupposes a background of common behaviour, as Wittgenstein pointed out.[28] His function seems more akin to that of a literary critic (one versed in the obscurantist grammar of Continental speculative philosophy, perhaps) who is unravelling the nuances, and building upon the content of, a poem or poetic statement. The only drawback here is that we have little knowledge of what it could be that the subject is casting in metaphor and imagery; by contrast, the successful destructuring of metaphor in poetry takes place against a background of minimally shared reference points. Since the subjects with whom Laing deals adduce descriptions of experiences that most of us (except, it seems, Laing himself) have lost, buried or become alienated from, we can only partake of the imaginings in our own way. Laing sets us two imagination tasks. There is the first-order task of making sense of the commentary of the former mental patient, and the second-order problem of seeing the correspondence between that and Laing's narrative supplementation. But we are left with unresolved ambiguities, logical problems and a strong sense of redundancy.

Laing makes the claim that we must cease to treat the diagnosed schizophrenic as a diseased organism and seek to facilitate his inner voyaging. This marks a break from his former cautious assertions about the limited generality of such voyaging (recall the repetitious : 'not always and not necessarily') amongst schizophrenics. Nonetheless, he proposes that if we did facilitate such trips into inner space we might learn more about our own, allegedly 'sane' existential situation, our 'being in the world'.[29] It is a generalised moral demand, announcing the need for a paradigm-switch in the psychiatric view of schizophrenia as a practical, medical problem. Laing and his colleagues (David Cooper and Aron Esterton) seek to substitute a  different moral order in society wherein the acts and utterances of persons formerly diagnosed as schizophrenic may be measured against different yardsticks of acceptability and intelligibility (although they have scarcely begun to think through the implications and repercussions of such a culture wide shift in morality and logic for activities and institutions *other than* those connected with formal psychiatric practice as currently conceived). They propose to replace the governing principle of psychiatric medicine as the expression of the 'technical interest' by principles expressing a version of the 'emancipatory interest,' in Habermas's terms.[30] Whether or not this is justifiable cannot be answered by appeal to science, phenomenology or the hermeneutic enterprise. One wonders how a shift in socially standardized vocabularies of motive might affect the institution of the 'Not guilty through insanity plea' in our legal system; if at present judge and jury will accept a plea 'only if they do not seem able to "understand" what could "cause" or *better motivate* a person to commit such and such a crime, i.e. if the deed appears pointless in terms of "commonsense" . . . '[31] as Devereux suggests, then in a future Laingian moral order might such a deed, committed by a diagnosed schizophrenic, be seen as part of his voyaging or an unpardonable deviation from it?

For an attempt to 'render intelligible' the ideas of diagnosed schizophrenics, Laing's interpretation itself poses problems of intelligibility. We are asked to substitute one level of unintelligibility by another; analyst and analysand both mystify us. In reconstructing the 'phenomenal world' of the patient, which in our terms means discussing aspects of his self-description, Laing gives the impression that his authority transcends that of mundane psychiatry or of psychoanalysis—he claims *privileged* insights which form the basis of a moral indictment of extant psychiatric practice. But there is no awareness of the problem of adequacy criteria in Laing's work; take any act, utterance, belief or reported experience and Laing can find some framework for incorporating it where society finds none. There is no sense of a problem of differentiating between *competing* accounts along principled lines. And, perhaps more significantly, there is little attention paid to the logical issue of when a statement ceases to be intelligible as a reason for an action or belief in any sense at all. Laing and his colleagues may try rhetorically to persuade us that such and such is a *good* reason for believing that one is, say, a computer or Jesus Christ or whatever, but there comes a limit beyond which a purported reason or explanation is simply unrecognizable *as* a reason or explanation.

There is a hiatus in Laing's work between his discussions of the nature of schizophrenic experiences and the sort of research he has undertaken on the 'transexperiential' social phenomenology of patients' families. In the former, we find an exclusive concentration upon the subject's inner territory, divorced from social determinations, and revealed in a sublanguage of 'ontological insecurity', 'sociobiological dysfunction', 'selfbody split' and so on, forming a loose mapping of psychic life. In the latter, intrafamilial experiences constitute the explanatory resource, framed in terms such as 'denials of autonomy and individuation'. Although he makes use of the work of Bateson, Lidz and the experiential aetiologists, he disavows an aetiological perspective for his own work, thus leaving us to choose between his mystical 'demystification' of the individual patient and his sociological 'contextualization' of the same. Writing with Aron Esterton in the Preface to the Second Edition of their *Sanity, Madness and the Family*,[32] Laing replies to critics of their first edition thus :

> Eleven cases, it is said, all women, prove nothing. There are no controls. How do you sample your data? What objective, reliable rating scales have you employed? And so on. Such criticism would be justified if we had set out to test the hypothesis that the family is a pathogenic variable in the genesis of schizophrenia. But we did not set out to do this, and we have not claimed to have done so. We set out to illustrate by eleven examples that, if we look at some experience and behaviour without reference to family

interactions, they may appear comparatively socially senseless, but that if we look at the same experience and behaviour in their original family context they are liable to make more sense.[33]

I am not sure whether we are meant to read this claim literally. If we are, then it is a very peculiar one indeed. It proposes that we could take any conduct or articulated experiences by a mental patient in any (unspecified) context of occurrence and recast it (perhaps by mental experimentation) within a family setting, thereby making it appear sensible. But the point is that if anyone behaves in any extraneous setting as if he were still operating in his family group, we should certainly think his conduct incongruous and perhaps feel him eligible for the ascription of insanity—it would hardly excuse such incongruence to 'think it into' some appropriate setting. I think Laing and Esterton are proposing that we construe 'schizophrenic' conduct and self-description as responses to, or products of, family-induced disorientation or dislocation. Inasmuch as this latter rendition seems reasonable, I cannot see how they can escape a quasi-aetiological perspective. The insane person is no longer 'irradiated with light from other worlds,'[34] but the miserable and confused result of intra-familial relationships of a distorting, debilitating kind. The patient is not alone in his disorientation—the family as a whole is implicated in madness, although Laing and Esterton refrain from extending the scope of application of the term in that way. Laing, in another paper,[35] makes it clear that he does not want to portray the family as the surrogate for the patient; the family itself is to be placed

> . . . within the context of its encompassing networks. These further networks must be seen within the contexts of yet larger organiz-ations and institutions. These larger contexts do not exist out there on some periphery of social space : they pervade the interstices of all that is comprised by them.[36]

The family is the mediator of an insane system of society; it inhabits a deranged social world, and no therapeutic manipulation within a family or post-hospital, social work intervention in the family situation of a patient can accommodate this state of affairs. The only solution is total social transformation. By both routes, by concentrating on the need to foster conditions favourable to existential voyaging and by focusing on the internal dynamics of debilitating family interaction, Laing reaches the same revolutionary conclusion. Most of what I have said about family interaction studies appears applicable to the details and framework of the Laing-Esterton study, and I think I have said enough about the thoroughgoing rhetorical foundations of Laing's phenomenology. There are no details of the sort of society which Laing would like to see established; would it feature the abolition of practical psychiatry and replace it with gurus guiding people through their explorations of self, or is it envisaged to create some form of societal disalienation of which everyone could partake?

Laing, Esterton and Cooper share with the more orthodox students of family interaction the idea that what we sometimes constitute as 'symptoms' or 'mere behaviour' on the part of a 'schizophrenic patient' are, in fact, sometimes strategically adopted or consciously chosen courses of action. Bert Kaplan, in his introduction to his edited collection of autobiographical accounts by ex mental patients, also subscribes to this view:

> The 'illness' is something the individual 'wills' to happen. Rather than belonging to a foreign process which has seized him, it belongs to him, and exists squarely within his region of responsibility. The term action is very well suited for expressing this idea. Action is something the person 'does'. It carries the connotation that a particular course of action is one that the person has 'chosen' and that he supports with his own energy.[37]

It seems to me that this could stand as a description of a fraud pretending or playing at mental disorder rather than someone actually mentally disordered. If we adopt this perspective, we are deprived of the means whereby we might differentiate between fakers and genuinely insane people. It is dangerous to the extent that it imputes responsibility to the conduct of the insane where humane laws have rescinded such imputation. And it is virtually incoherent in that insanity is partially definable as something that *happens to* someone; if someone whom we believe insane is found not to be 'doing what comes naturally,' then we may very well revise our view of him to something like 'malicious jester' or worse. Clearly, insanity happens to people in a different way to the sort of 'happening' involved in getting a cold or contracting a physical disease. But if a case of insanity is genuine, it cannot be a chosen course of action. Sometimes, as Braginsky, Braginsky and Ring have shown,[38] people display 'symptoms' in order to get into a mental hospital as a refuge or shelter; they use 'symptoms' as 'tickets of admission'. But such people, whilst being social problems, stand in definite contrast to those who become convinced of some unsupportable belief or fantasy and get referred to an institution and hospitalized as a result. One does not *choose* to believe that one is persecuted by the Freemasons, Communist Party or Martian invaders in the sense that one rationally considers alternatives when one is insane—one simply is convinced without any reason at all, or a reason so peculiar and tortuous that it defies rational examination and investigation. Deliberate phantasizing and experiential experimentation may well occur amongst quite sound, rational people; but there are limits. Insane people are sometimes *preoccupied with* phantasizing to the exclusion of all mundane functioning, and it is no use telling them that they are selecting a way of life which could culminate in the loss of civil life and comparative freedom of action. Much of the talk about the insane, 'schizophrenic' cognisance of his self-presentations and performances stems from the misapplication of the concept of 'insight', and the related notion that, because a patient may articulate the occasional sensible remark or manage to do some set of tasks competently, then he is *basically* sane and sound. I have already suggested that the existence of such sypmtomatological discontinuities should be investigated as counter-evidence to the assumption that all of the heterogeneous populations diagnosed as schizophrenic are suffering from an organic dysfunction; but it cannot be assumed that, because a patient or group of patients are not wholly unable to function, therefore they are not really insane or mentally disordered.

The concept of 'insight' is used in psychiatry and psychiatric social work in two ways. Firstly, it depicts the ability of some patients to construe themselves as 'ill' or 'sick', i.e. to define their situation in terms conducive to psychiatric treatment. Secondly, and more restrictedly, it depicts the ability of some patients to theorize about, to reflect upon and stand at a distance from their problems and preoccupations. However, sometimes the use of the concept in this latter sense tempts users to generalize out into a fullblown redefinition of the patient, a redefinition which is based upon partial considerations and usually forged without regard to the contingencies which motivated the original committal. This is not to say that whenever a patient is possessed of such 'insight' no one has the right to see in that a spill-over into overall normality and to press for discharge on that basis. Rather, I am suggesting that bits of evidence about sane functioning cannot stand on their own as grounds for redefinition; a psychopathic killer may well be able to read a newspaper and light a cigarette, a schizophrenic may well be found writing long stories in coherent English and mending a radio set (both clinical examples that are well known), but only in the light of a more complete assessment could a redefinition of psychological status be commonsensically as well as psychiatrically warranted.

Laing notes that one diagnosed schizophrenic once stated:

> We schizophrenics say and do a lot of stuff that is unimportant, and then we mix important things in with all this to see if the doctor cares enough to see them and feel them.[39]

And again:

> The problem with schizophrenics is that they can't trust anyone. They can't put their eggs in one basket. The doctor will usually have to fight to get in no matter how much the patient objects. It is wonderful to be beaten up or killed because no one ever does that to you unless they really care and can be made very upset....[40]

If we suppress detailed considerations of content, these remarks appear at once articulate, reflective and coherent. Admitting a little of the content into view, we become intrigued to read of a diagnosed schizophrenic employing the psychiatric classificatory concept to herself—'insight' *par excellence*. But when we pause to take stock of the implicativeness of what was said, we find in it an almost child-like concern at being noticed, at being important, at belonging to someone, a concern taken to extreme lengths in the former (in that the patient feels that she and her fellow inmates must resort to covert tactics to test the concern and care of the doctor) and in the latter (where being the subject of someone's violence is seen as 'wonderful' and a token of positive feelings in the absence of any other expression of such feelings). Laing cannot have it both ways; either he must use these citations as evidence in favour of his unilateral redefinition of the psychological status of these speakers, and engage in a synecdochal assessment of the type I criticized above, or he must read off from these citations evidence of a pathetic feeling of insignificance in keeping with an assessment of mental incompetence in a wider sense. I doubt very much whether the former reading would impress a clinical psychiatrist of other than a Laingian persuasion; it certainly doesn't permit of only one interpretation favourable to the speakers. My own version, or 'hearing', leads me to wonder about the mental state of the producers of these remarks; being as charitable as possible, I cannot see that if a mental patient said such things in all seriousness then he or she was wrongly hospitalized.

Evidence of some degree of cognisance, of reflective thinking capacity, cannot stand alone as evidence of the sanity of someone legitimately hospitalized as insane. Many persons labelled as 'paranoid' are both garrulous and coherent, sometimes studious and of obvious intelligence. Laing cites another patient, Rose, who describes some of her experiences in these terms :

> . . . my head's full of thoughts, fears, hates, jealousies. My head can't grip them; I can't hold on to them. I'm behind the bridge of my nose—I mean, my consciousness is there. They're splitting open my head, oh, that's schizophrenic, isn't it?[41]

The girl circumscribes one clause as characteristically 'schizophrenic' —but what about the rest of her description? Are we to impute insight and rationality on the basis of her last whole utterance and omit reference to the peculiarity of what preceded it? Clearly, 'schizophrenic episodes' are not all of a piece, and Goffman has done some disservice with his idea that in total institutions there can arise total transformations of self. Both ideas : the homogeneity of the patient's 'disease process' and the homogeneity of the patient's 'institutionalization', distort our thinking about madness.

In the Kaplan collection, Norma MacDonald writes about her experiences of 'Living with Schizophrenia'.[42] She retrospectively pieces together what happened to her whilst at the same time recalling how she lacked control over most of the process. In the famous account, 'The Autobiography of a Schizophrenic Experience', the subject recalls how she *drifted into* her period of acute dislocation from her daily life.[43] Neither seems reconcilable with Kaplan's (and Laing's) stress on choice, strategy and all-pervading cognisance. It is quite true that some psychiatrists and psychopathologists use the concept of 'thought disorder' in a similar way to that in which a physician uses the concept of arteriosclerotic dementia. The psychiatrist may well find that such a use, whilst obviously glossing the diversity of manifestation of word salads and the like, enables him to effect a categorization that suffices for his practical purposes. The psychopathologist, however, cannot use such a concept in such a way as an item in his theoretical armoury; he risks homogenizing and objectifying complex processes too easily. The phenomenologist need only draw attention to the inner complexity of 'thought-process disorder' to rebut such glib objectifications. Ritson and Forrest,[44] in a paper on the simulation of psychosis, gave an account of one subject who would 'turn on' his word salad or 'schizophrenese' whenever the psychiatric consultant was showing students around the ward, and of another patient (an American postgraduate student) who alternated between speaking 'schizophrenese' and routine English. (Norman Cameron remarked that: ". . . in the asyndesis of schizophrenia we are dealing with a process that may become reversible."[45]) Having said that, however, we are in no position to infer that such patients are not really insane or 'thought-disordered', nor are we in a position to decode everything they say as if they were engaged in continuous, strategic punning. It is quite possible to construe what many diagnosed schizophrenics say as nonsense without thereby vouchsafing the integrity of the medical model of mental disease in psychopathology.

Phenomenologists are right to indicate the source of much distortion in our knowledge of insanity in the unfounded extension of the use of the medical gnosology. However, as I have tried to show, much of their own theorizing is undisciplined, speculative and occasionally incoherent. In trying to escape society's puzzlement with the enigma of non-organic insanity, they often seek refuge in esoteric constructions whose relationship to the phenomena is hard to discern at every point, and their emphasis upon 'intentionality' and 'existentiality' stems from the attempt to elevate insanity into a hitherto undeciphered form of sanity, perhaps of a higher order, in which the grounds of action and experience are not available to ordinary people in a society. Whilst it is true that the indiscriminate use of the disease concept can put an end to the development of microscopic analyses of individual cases, and can thereby inhibit the development of rigorous, clinical descriptions that contribute to our understanding of the nature of such cases, it is also true that the indiscriminate use of unclarified conceptual frameworks hinders the understanding we seek in our own logic.

The rhetoric of decipherment appears in a recent paper by the German sociologist, Jurgen Habermas.[46] Drawing on the work of Alfred Lorenzer,[47] Habermas conceives of psychoanalytic encounters in terms of translation rules and decoding practices. The subject or patient is thought of as the bearer of a private, pre-linguistic symbol organisation which emerges publicly as 'systematically distorted communication' that gets labelled 'symptomatic behaviour'. In a psychoanalytic encounter, pathological speech is 'decoded' through a process termed 'scenic understanding' wherein the analyst is presumed to :

> . . . resolve confusions of ordinary speech by interpreting them either as forced regression back to an earlier level of communication, or as the breakthrough of the earlier form of communication into language.[48]

A childhood trauma causes the child to desymbolize the reference person in the traumatic situation, and the 'vacancy' in the 'semantic field' is closed by employing some other symbol which has sense only for the subject. The analyst aims at the achievement of resymbolization (the re-entry of the suppressed symbolic contents into public communication). The repertoire of publicly communicable symbols is populated with ordinary semantics and with 'paleosymbols' deployed as defence mechanisms against the intrusion of the excommunicated ones. These 'paleosymbols' are 'archaic' and prelinguistic. As such, they can only be determined through the analysis of data on dreams and speech pathology. Systematically distorted communication 'can be explained by the fact that paleosymbolically fixed semantic contents have encysted themselves like foreign bodies into the grammatically regulated use of symbols.'[49] Paleosymbols control interaction; they are not just signs. A transfer of the 'semantic contents from the prelinguistic into the linguistic aggregate conditions widens the scope of communicative action at the cost of unconsciously motivated action.'[50] This transfer is a kind of 'liberation'; it occurs in our reaction to jokes, as well.

I have tried not to misstate Habermas' position here, although I found it both confusing and confused. Confining myself to the above sketch, certain issues immediately present themselves. The first is the assumption of a process of 'desymbolization'—is this more than a metaphorical way of reporting the fact that children sometimes forget painful experiences, or cannot bring themselves to talk openly about them, or talk about them in idiosyncratic ways so as to avoid open contemplation of the full recollection of the experience or situation in question? It seems to me doubtful that it is more than such a metaphor, but a troublesome one since it broadens out into an account of a prelinguistic level of cognition comprising private semantic contents. This is clearly reminiscent of the private language argument about sensations, although a little different in certain details. However, I don't think it different enough to withstand the sort of rebuttal Wittgenstein offered against the private language idea. Basically, a language containing symbols whose sense is wholly private could not be taught, and as such would not really be a language in the usual sense. Moreover, how could one sustain a privately meaningful use or reference without external checks which could assure that one had, in fact, made the correct identifications as opposed to merely *thinking* that one had? Again, if one thought in prelinguistic terms, how could one be sure that $X$ was a *correct* translation of one's prelinguistic thought contents into words of a public language, as opposed to merely *believing* it correct?

Paleosymbols are apparently prelinguistic; yet further on we are told that psychoanalytic language analysis dealing with pathological speech disturbances has the duty of dissolving this syndrome, i.e. of isolating the two language levels.[51] At first, we had prelinguistic symbols; now a level of *language*. Earlier, we read that a transfer of prelinguistic semantics (sic) to the general conditions of linguistic communication was the goal of analysis (with no specification of how anything prelinguistic could have semantic content); now, we are told that the goal is the isolation of two language levels. What does all this signify? An answer—tentatively suggested—might be that Habermas is trying to unify Freudian theory and practice with the contemporary stress on language as the vehicle of thought in communication theory. The Freudian unconscious is peopled with paleosymbols; the consciousness with ordinary linguistic and other socially-derived and socially-sustained symbolic contents. The 'unconscious' is, as Louch had it, a category of analysis which 'eases the strain on the concept of strategy, when that concept is extended to include the actions of the mentally ill'.[52] It is also conceptualized as a repository, usually of motives. The only trouble with this is that a motive does not occur in a particular time and place (where and when could we locate my motive for assaulting the man who insulted my wife when I don't even perform the act of assault?) Sometimes, motive talk is suspended in favour of 'drive' talk, and a rapid degeneration into biological reductionism is inevitable. There seems little point in resurrecting the arguments against the idea of 'unconsciously motivated action' which Habermas uses; the assumption that everything I do has a motive, even if I cannot avow it, has long been discredited, and is the source for Freud's postulate.

The ideas of the 'unconscious' and the 'phenomenal world' inform, respectively, psychoanalysis and phenomenological psychopathology. In the former, the supposition that the acquisition of language, knowledge and experience requires a psychic warehouse as well as the physiological equipment for reproducing such knowledge, using a language and recollecting such experiences, underlies the concept of mental zones of which the unconscious is one. Freud considered that, since we are not all the time aware of the totality of our knowledge and experience, then there must be some realm in which they are stored away. He assimilated the acquisition of knowledge and experience to the grammar of acquisition of material possessions. Of course, as White[53] and others have shown, the question; 'Where is my knowledge when I am not recalling it?' stems from such a grammatical misassimilation, and can be compared to an equivalent misassimilation; 'Where is my conceit when I am not displaying it?' Latency does not imply locality. In the latter, phenomenological conception, it is often assumed (especially in the use of the notion of 'phenomenalization') that because we recognize things in our environment by their look, sound, smell, taste and feel, we begin by describing their phenomenal properties and work outwards to infer their real properties from their phenomenal ones. As Place remarked,[54] the reverse is the case :

> We begin by learning to recognise the real properties of things in our environment. We learn to recognise them, of course by their look, sound, smell, taste, and feel; but this does not mean that we have to learn to describe the look, sound, smell, taste, and feel of things before we can describe the things themselves. Indeed, it is only after we have learned to describe the things in our environment that we can learn to describe our consciousness of them.[55]

Our descriptive protocols are predicted upon our learning about the things in our environment, and it is only where such protocols appear inappropriate to the situation that we issue them with qualificatory phrases such as 'it appears', 'seems', 'looks', 'feels', etc. If *all* our descriptive protocols were cast in such terms *(per impossibile)* then the idea of multiple phenomenal fields or phenomenal worlds might seem more generally applicable. As things are, the employment of such terminology can lead to a confusion in which we are supposed never to be able to describe real objects and processes in the real world—only experiential objects in a phenomenal world. Data from mental patients, whose descriptions of experience do not seem to us to be descriptions of real things in the world, are used as the basis for a general scepticism about all other descriptions founded on sense perception. The fact that there can be a multiplicity of ways of describing some scene or event is conjoined to the fact that some people describe scenes and events in terms disjunctive with our ordinary standards of description to issue in a theory, not of multiple accounts, but of multiple *realities*. Nothing can be proposed as unreal or illusory—it is simply part of a *different* reality; that of, say, a schizophrenic patient. This perspective so distorts the morality of our ordinary thinking and inferring that it is rarely sustained consistently by its advocates, and could not possibly inform our conduct in the world. There could not be a language in which there is no agreed way of distinguishing the real from the unreal. If our experiences were wholly unique, no communication could obtain between us.

Phenomenologists who propose to 'describe the world as it presents itself to consciousness' often approach their task as if their descriptions so formulated should *in principle* be distinct from descriptions of the world period. Users of the notion of 'phenomenal world' or 'phenomenal field' (such as Snygg and Combs,[56] Carl Rogers,[57] R. B. MacLeod[58] and others) differ in their orientation but agree on the generality of the distinction 'objective/phenomenal'. This rests, as I have suggested, on taking descriptive protocols such as : 'it appears to be . . .' or 'it looks like . . .' as paradigms for all descriptive protocols, whereas they are limiting cases and depend for their sense and use on the prior sense and use of unqualified descriptions of objects and processes in the world.

Given the limitations on the applicability of experiential protocols, I think we can begin to see where they might apply usefully. In dealing with hallucinatory experiences, for example, the phenomenologist is indeed in a position to argue that there is something distinct about the way in which the data of consciousness (or experience) can be described.

Hallucinations are often taken to be criterial of chronic schizophrenia; most of the organic researches (and at least one non-organic account as well)[59] which focus upon 'schizophrenia' actually deal with hallucinatory experiences. A hallucination is a sense dependent percept. It is a percept whose status is denied intersubjectivity; i.e. it is denied any 'external, objective correlate' in the environment by other people. Frequently, the distinctions between a hallucination, an illusion, a delusion, a vision, a daydream, an eidetic image and an imagining are blurred, and without this prior conceptual separation, discussion of hallucinatory experiences becomes problematic and confusing. Psychopathologists do not always separate out these phenomena—perhaps because practising psychiatrists don't, either—but as theoreticians accounting for phenomena they have less excuse than psychiatrists making an ad hoc ascription or ratification of 'hallucinations' in the conduct of their everyday work.

It is clear that a person who reported having had an hallucinatory experience could only distinguish between that and the normal operations of his sensory perceptual faculties if he held *independent beliefs* that enabled him to sort out the status of his perceptions. The same is the case for illusions. A man might undergo a mescaline induced hallucination and observe a conjuror levitate his assistant, but in neither case, the hallucination or the illusion, need he be mistaken or deceived about the real nature of things. Illusions (such as the already mentioned Müller-Lyer illusion) are distortions in the visual field of real objects, and they are determinable as such by way of further investigations, checks and yardsticks. Hallucinations, by contrast, are not simply misinterpretations of perceived phenomena (phenomena that can be discerned by others, actually or potentially) but are wholly subjective. A delusion can inform the interpretation of real, intersubjectively available objects and processes in such a way that, as Kraepelin remarked,[60] we might confuse a deluded interpretation of real perceptions with an account of a hallucination. But there is a clear distinction to be drawn between such a confusion and genuine cases of hallucination, even if psychiatrists are not always careful to sort them out. A delusion, in itself, is a species of mistaken factual belief—a socially unsupported aberration of belief. It makes sense to suppose that a person continuously subjected to hallucinations might frame some delusion around them, or construct some system of fantasy to incorporate their recurrence, but it is not plausible to suggest that being deluded leads on to being hallucinated automatically. The conflation of 'delusion' with 'hallucination' is quite common amongst mental health personnel, but the relationship between the two is analysable. Sometimes, the phenomena of religious visions is cited in order to demonstrate the connection between a type of belief and hallucinations, but this only works if we can be persuaded to treat visions as hallucinations in the first place. A vision is a kind of percept whose status is informed by established beliefs; only a religious man can have a vision of the Virgin Mary or the

Archangel Gabriel, whereas a non-religious man who saw either would think that he had an hallucination (unless, of course, it inspired a religious conversion in him, in which case he might *retrospectively* constitute it as a divine vision). If we wish to sustain our doubts about the beliefs espoused by religious people, we might well refer to *all* divine visions as hallucinations, but in doing so we would be arguing against the *special status* of the visions, and not, I think, against the distinction between percepts informed by special beliefs and percepts not so informed. (By 'informed' here, I mean something like 'contingent upon,' but a more precise specification escapes me.) Not every hallucinatory experience undergone by a cleric could be intelligibly scored up to divinity. Finally, there are daydreams, eidetic projections and vivid imaginings. A daydream rarely has the qualities normally attributed to hallucinations, e.g. 'objective outthereness', and more importantly, daydreaming is something that people *do,* hallucinating is something that *happens.* One cannot start and stop a hallucination, and one cannot control its occurrence and features; one can decide to indulge in daydreaming, but one cannot decide to have a hallucination. Eidetic images and projections are a species of after-image (e.g. you look hard at a well-illuminated figure and then close your eyes and still see it), and although fantastic eidetic images have been recorded, Kandinsky rightly insisted that they were 'pseudo-hallucinations'. Vivid imaginings are similar to daydreams in that they are not passively witnessed but actively produced (or, at least, although one could be said to 'drift into' daydreams, one is still intelligibly described as *doing* something; the same in the case of imagining). One does not 'undergo' a daydream or an imagining as one might undergo a hallucinatory experience. And, of course, hallucinations may be auditory and tactile as well as visual. (This is something often conveniently overlooked by biochemists who seek to posit hallucinogenic drugs as analogues of pathogenic metabolites in mental disorders—it is very rare for the hallucinator whose percepts are drug-induced to experience auditory or tactile hallucinations, whilst it is more common amongst diagnosed schizophrenics to have these latter sorts of hallucination).

The French psychiatrist, Guiraud, writing in the early nineteenth century, produced a set of rules for the 'correct identification' of hallucinations amongst mentally disordered persons, and Vernon worked with them in his research on sensory deprivation.[61] Vernon inventoried them as follows:

(1) The experience must have an 'out-thereness', just like any visual experience of the real world, (2) the one experiencing the hallucination must be able to scan, to attend selectively to, the various parts of the experience, (3) it must not be producible at the will of the subject, (4) the subject must not be able to terminate it, and (5) it must, for all purposes, 'fool' the observer with its realism.[62]

Apart from (5), which presupposes the absence of independent beliefs which could enable the subject to discriminate between hallucinatory and non-hallucinatory percepts, this list of rules reiterates some of the important *conceptual* distinctions to be drawn in the case of describing what could count in the category of hallucinatory experiences. Clinicians rarely go in for such intricate probing of their subjects' accounts, and yet the distinctions remain important because they *can* be made. Sarbin, one of the few theoreticians to approach the problem of hallucinations and their recognition from a position *outside* medical-psychiatric gnosology, has this to say :

> The term hallucination is pejorative. It is generally applied to the reported imaginings of people already considered degraded . . . the term hallucination does not point to a special class of imaginings. Rather, the term in practice is pejorative, coterminous with madness, lunacy and schizophrenia. That some reported imaginings are neutrally valued, or even positively valued as in poetry and prose, cannot be gainsaid. So we cannot place a negatively laden value term on imaginings per se . . . no determinate tests are available for distinguishing between reported imaginings to which a non-pejorative label may be applied and to reported imaginings to which the pejorative 'hallucination' is applied.[63]

Sarbin does not consider in the above the known relationship between certain neurotoxic conditions (such as encephalitis lethargica) and the constant reportage by victims of bizarre percepts and auditory hallucinations, nor the known relationship between certain neurologically active drugs like LSD-25 (which over-accelerates the release of transmitter fluid in the brain) and the experience of hallucinations, nor the large amount of work done on sensory deprivation. Since he confines himself to hallucinations amongst the mentally disordered, his over-generalized assertion about the 'pejorative' sense of the word is misplaced. He is right to point out that at any time the labelling of an imagining as hallucination can follow only from a chain of inferences. 'Data are not immediately given. Rather, they must be filtered through the beliefs and values of the diagnoser;'[64] he is also right to note that there are many cases where first person psychological statements from the subject or patient are not forthcoming but the ascription of hallucinatory experiences is still made. But he is wrong when he proposes that the term 'hallucination' does not point to a special class of imaginings as if that were decisive in proving his point that the term is exclusively pejorative. Hallucinations, as I have argued, are not imaginings at all; they are conceptually quite distinct.

Sarbin considers that accounts of what we call 'hallucinations', given by patients or candidates for mental hospitalization, are in fact accounts of real objects and processes formulated as compressed similes; the subjects offering the accounts fail to articulate the crucial qualifier, 'as if'.[65] Hallucinations are ascribed on the basis of faulty inferences from linguistic communications in which such qualifiers are omitted. This thesis, then, constitutes a radical rejection of the whole concept of 'hallucination' as a pejorative gambit deployed against already labelled subjects on the basis of their consistently metaphoric speech practices.

It is certainly true that claiming drug free hallucinatory experiences does not automatically engender ascriptions of insanity; sometimes the claims are prefaced with appropriate disclaimers such as 'I know this sounds crazy, but . . .', and 'This is impossible, I know, but . . .' and the like. Conversely, already labelled persons (those whose psychological status is already in doubt or open to question) and especially former mental patients who remark on some unusual visual or auditory experience may well find themselves attributed with hallucinations, or a 'relapse' into a hallucinatory condition. Yet it is quite far-fetched to suppose that someone quite sane who made some remark or series of remarks of a compressed, elliptical or metaphorical nature about real objects or processes in the world could be socially stigmatized and even hospitalized as insane on that basis. Not only does this presuppose that such a person lacked the capacity to make clear how his remarks had been intended once it became clear that they had been so seriously (and stupidly) misconstrued by some audience, but it presupposes that all cases in which lay and professional persons ascribe hallucinations are of the kind that succumb to analysis in terms of such misconstruction. There are clearly practical tests for determining whether or not someone merely has an elliptical, imagery-strewn manner of talking or is in fact recounting or making allusion to hallucinatory experiences of some sort. Sarbin simply fails to concretize his abstract portrayal of the ascription process—so divorced is it from the practical facts of interactional dealings between people that it obfuscates the tactics and strategies that are quite mundanely available to people in everyday life for making the determinations Sarbin thinks are not made, or not even possible. Indeed, to ascribe hallucinations to someone who does not actually state a first person claim to them is to make an ascription of the last resort, i.e. when all other options are proven untenable in the case at hand. Moreover, those cases for which a clinician has good grounds in maintaining the label of 'hallucinated' are cases in which the content of the reported percepts defies unpacking as a simile or metaphor except in the most abstruse and idiosyncratic sense.

One way of making some sense out of Sarbin's perspective is to treat it as an expression of the point made by Kraepelin, and cited earlier, that quite often clinicians tend to confuse or conflate delusional misinterpretations of real perceptions with hallucinations. If we suspend consideration of that part of Sarbin's thesis in which he attempts to assimilate all cases of reported hallucination to cases of linguistic compression and ellipsis, we can read it as an extension of Kraepelin's point. But, as I suggested, this has relevance only where naïve aetiological researchers allow busy clinicians to generate their samples of 'hallucinated subjects' for them; it does not threaten the integrity of the concept of 'hallucination' and its genuine use in describing aspects of mental disorder for practical purposes.

In dealing with hallucinations, I have tried to show that a conceptual disentanglement enables us to discern the nature (or perhaps the 'essence'?) of the phenomenon of hallucination more rigorously than eidetic-reductive speculations of a phenomenological type.

In conclusion : phenomenological speculations on insanity fail to convince us on conceptual and empirical grounds. The rhetorical claims far outstrip the value of the phenomenological enterprise in psychopathology as conceived by Laing and his colleagues. The conceptualization of insanity as willed action developed by Kaplan was found untenable, and the conceptualization of speech disturbances in mental disorder as the emergence of a level of paleo-symbolic communication proposed by Habermas was found incoherent. The concept of the 'phenomenal world' and 'phenomenal field' used in some phenomenological accounts was discussed and criticized, and the experiential field of hallucinations was dealt with in a manner that contrasted with phenomenological speculation.

Rather than attempt to uncover the mythic 'essences' or a priori, apodictic truths about phenomena as a basis for the natural sciences, in the manner of the classic phenomenological programme, I tried to show by example how conceptual-analytic work prepares the ground for empirical investigation more adequately and with fewer debatable claims for its products. How far I succeeded in this with my discussion of hallucinations is, of course, for the reader to decide. But I think that any adequate rebuttal of my analytical distinctions can only derive from the same source—conceptual or logical investigation of the grammar of our linguistic terms, and not from any undisciplined inner rumination.

## NOTES

1.   Edmund Husserl *Phenomenology and the Crisis of Philosophy* New York, Harper Torchbooks (1965) p. 92. See also his *Crisis of the European Sciences and Transcendental Phenomenology (Die Krisis der Europäischen Wissenschaften und die transzendentale Phänomenologie)* The Hague, Husserliana (1954)

2.   Gilbert Ryle 'Phenomenology versus "The Concept of Mind" ' in his *Collected Papers, vol. 1: Critical Essays* Hutchinson (1971) p. 179. See also Ryle's earlier paper, also reproduced in this collection, entitled 'Phenomenology' (ibid., pp. 167-78). It may seem odd to cite from Ryle, whose intellectual development has been away from phenomenology, as an authority on the same. However, I have found Ryle's exposition both fair and concise, and, in characteristic fashion, immensely insightful.

3.   The essay is the one entitled 'Phenomenology' cited above.

4.   E. Husserl *Ideas* Allen & Unwin (1967) pp. 261-2

5.   Gilbert Ryle 'Phenomenology versus "The Concept of Mind" ' op. cit. p. 189. In a later essay (in the collection, not chronologically) Ryle, reviewing Farber's *The Foundations of Phenomenology*, speaks of the 'flat impropriety' of asserting that one could 'peer at Remorse', 'gaze at Induction', 'take a long look at Choice' or 'happen to light on Conscience' (op. cit. p. 220) in the way in which the Husserlian programme for the essentialistic investigation into mental functioning would suggest. We elucidate such mental concepts not by gazing at the wearers of linguistic terms but by fixing the parameters of their logical behaviour in mundane discourse.

6.   Maurice Merleau-Ponty 'What is Phenomenology?' in J. Kockelmans (ed.) *Phenomenology* New York, Anchor Books (1967) p. 356. For a slightly different translation, see the same essay in Jerry H. Gill (ed.) *Philosophy*

*Today, No. 3* Macmillan (1970) p. 17 et seq

7. Aron Gurvitsch 'The Phenomenological and the Psychological Approach to Consciousness' in Maurice Natanson (ed.) *Essays in Phenomenology* The Hague, Nijhoff (1966) pp. 40-46

8. R. B. MacLeod 'Phenomenology: A Challenge to Experimental Psychology' in T. W. Wann (ed.) *Behaviorism and Phenomenology* Phoenix, The University of Chicago Press (1967) pp. 47-74. I discuss this conception later in the chapter.

9. D. Katz *Die Erscheinungsweisen der Farben* Leipzig, J. A. Barth (1911); cited in MacLeod, op. cit. pp. 59-60

10. R. B. MacLeod, op. cit. p. 60

11. M. Merleau-Ponty *The Structure of Behaviour* Boston, Beacon Press (1963)

12. J. S. Bruner and C. C. Goodman 'Value and Need as Organising Factors in Perception' *Journal of Abnormal and Social Psychology* vol. 42 (1947) pp. 33-44

13. Karl Jaspers 'The Phenomenological Approach in Psychopathology' *British Journal of Psychiatry* vol. 114 (1968) pp. 1313-23. Originally, 'Die phänomenologische Forschungsrichtung in der Psychopathologie' *Zeit. Neur.* vol. 9 (1912). In this paper, traces of a Husserlian essentialism remain in the discussion of 'subjective irreducibles.'

14. Karl Jaspers, *General Psychopathology* trans. J. Hoening and Marian W. Hamilton, Manchester University Press (1962)

15. ibid p. 56

16. ibid p. 581

17. R. D. Laing *The Divided Self* Pelican (1969) Chapter Two

18. ibid p. 31

19. Hugo Meynell 'Philosophy and Schizophrenia' *The Journal of the British Society for Phenomenology* Vol. 2 No. 2 (May 1971) pp. 17-30

20. R. D. Laing op. cit. p. 28

21. ibid p. 28

22. R. D. Laing *The Politics of Experience and The Bird of Paradise* Penguin (1968) p. 102. In this discussion, I make no reference to the latter section of the book *The Bird of Paradise.*

23. ibid pp. 120-37

24. ibid p. 123

25. ibid p. 136. This teleological conception involves the kind of organicist metaphor which Laing disavowed in his preface to the 1970 Pelican edition of his collaborative work, *Sanity, Madness and the Family.*

26. R. D. Laing *The Divided Self* op. cit. Chapter Four

27. R. D. Laing *The Politics of Experience* op. cit. p. 125

28. Ludwig Wittgenstein *Philosophical Investigations* trans. G. E. M. Anscombe, Oxford, Basil Blackwell (1968) para. 206: 'The common behaviour of mankind is the system of reference by means of which we interpret an unknown language.'

29. L. Binswanger *Being in the World* New York, Basic Books (1963)

30. Jurgen Habermas 'Knowledge and Interest' *Inquiry* vol. 9 (1966) pp. 285-300. The technical 'interest' is the research-governing motivation

pertaining to the production of knowledge used for manipulation and control. The emancipatory 'interest' is the research-governing motivation pertaining to the production of critical-ethical-humanistic theory.

31. G. Devereux 'Two Types of Modal Personality Models' in *Studying Personality Cross-Culturally* Evanstone; Row, Peterson & Co (1961) Chapter 6 p. 235

32. R. D. Laing and Aron Esterton *Sanity, Madness and the Family* Pelican (1970). The first edition was published in 1964 by Tavistock.

33. ibid p. 12. The chief critic of the original work along the lines mentioned in the citation was probably John K. Wing in his article 'A Review of *Sanity, Madness and the Family' New Society* vol. 84 (7 May 1964) pp. 23-4.

34. R. D. Laing *The Politics of Experience* op. cit. p. 114

35. R. D. Laing 'The Obvious' in David Cooper (ed.) *The Dialectics of Liberation* Penguin (1968)

36. ibid p. 15

37. Bert Kaplan (ed.) 'Introduction' to *The Inner World of Mental Illness* Harper & Row (1964) p. x

38. R. Braginsky, Braginsky & Ring *Methods of Madness: The Mental Hospital as a Last Resort* New York, Holt, Rinehart & Winston (1969)

39. R. D. Laing, *The Divided Self* Pelican (1969) p. 164

40. ibid p. 167

41. ibid p. 151

42. Norma MacDonald 'Living with Schizophrenia' *Canadian Medical Association Journal* 23 January 1960, reproduced in full in B. Kaplan (ed.) op. cit. pp. 173-84

43. Anonymous 'An Autobiography of a Schizophrenic Experience' *Journal of Abnormal and Social Psychology* vol. 51 (1955) pp. 677-89, reproduced in full in B. Kaplan (ed.), op. cit. pp. 89-115

44. Bruce Ritson and Alistair Forrest 'The Simulation of Psychosis: A Contemporary Presentation' *British Journal of Medical Psychology* vol. 43 (March, 1970)

45. Norman Cameron 'Reasoning, Regression and Communication in Schizophrenics' in Max Hamilton (ed.) *Abnormal Psychology* Penguin (1967) p. 163

46. Jurgen Habermas 'On Systematically Distorted Communication' *Inquiry* vol. 13 No. 3 (Autumn 1970) pp. 205-18

47. Habermas uses a hitherto untranslated paper by Lorenzer, entitled 'Symbol und Verstehen im psychoanalytischen Prosen, Vorarbeiten zu einer Metatheorie der Psychoanalyse' Frankfurt (1970)

48. J. Habermas op. cit. p. 214

49. ibid Elsewhere in this paper, Habermas states that: 'distorted communication becomes noticeable because of the use of rules that deviate from the recognised system of linguistic rules.' This doubly over-intellectualizes the issues; in the first place, there is no 'recognised' system of linguistic rules beyond those which linguists are having trouble in codifying, and in the second place, distorted communication is distorted because it appears disorganized, e.g., hardly rule-guided in *any* sense.

50. ibid p. 215

51. ibid p. 215

52. A. R. Louch *Explanation and Human Action* Oxford, Basil Blackwell (1966) p. 228

53. Alan R. White *The Philosophy of Mind* New York, Random House (1967), p. 45

54. U. T. Place 'Is Consciousness a Brain Process?' in V. C. Chappell (ed.) *The Philosophy of Mind* Prentice-Hall (1962) pp. 101-109. My citing some of the ideas embodied in this paper does not commit me to the acceptance of the general thesis which is defended in it.

55. ibid p. 108

56. Donald Snygg and Arthur W. Combs *Individual Behaviour: A New Frame of Reference for Psychology* New York, Harper (1959)

57. Carl Rogers *Client-Centred Therapy* Boston (1951). See also his *On Becoming a Person* Boston (1961)

58. R. B. MacLeod 'Phenomenology: A Challenge to Experimental Psychology' in T. W. Wann (ed.) *Behaviourism and Phenomenology. Contrasting Bases for Modern Psychology* Phoenix/The University of Chicago Press (1964) esp. pp. 63-5

59. Paul McReynolds 'Anxiety, Perception and Schizophrenia' in D. D. Jackson (ed.) *The Aetiology of Schizophrenia* Basic Books (1960) pp. 248-92

60. E. Kraepelin, excerpts from his *Manic-Depressive Insanity and Paranoia* in Max Hamilton (ed.) *Abnormal Psychology* Penguin (1967) p. 74

61. Jack A. Vernon *Inside the Black Room: Studies of Sensory Deprivation* Pelican (1966) Chapter 11

62. ibid p. 119

63. T. Sarbin 'The Concept of Hallucination' *Journal of Personality* vol. 35 (1967) p. 379

64. ibid p 370

65. ibid. p 371

# PART TWO

# Culture and Psychological Ascription

# CHAPTER FOUR

# Insanity Ascription

## SECTION ONE : INTRODUCTION

I have sought to argue in the preceding chapters that the positivist
study of the schizophrenias is essentially bound up with conceptual
anomalies and methodological oddities. Organic aetiological theories
have all focused upon the possibility of the existence of pathogenic
metabolites or other lesions which might account for certain restricted
types of 'symptom', e.g. visual hallucinations, but have all claimed
the objective of generality to 'schizophrenia' or some other class of
'illness' and have thereby encountered great difficulty in replicat-
ing, or in deriving warrantable inferences from replications. (I have
outlined what I believe to be a more a !equate metatheoretical
perspective within which the organic interest might be located).
Psychogenic and sociogenic positivism have also been involved in
the framing of contrived and logically inappropriate frameworks of
conceptualization, and some studies of this type have required an
illicit redefinition of insane persons as more or less desperate
strategists presenting themselves *as* insane for ulterior purposes. The
phenomenological intervention of the Tavistock clinicians has only
succeeded in obscuring a number of critical issues (many of which
they were instrumental in raising) by confusion and polemic, and
this has undoubtedly hindered the development of non-positivistic
alternatives to orthodox psychopathology.

We must, I believe, redefine the sociologist's legitimate interest in
the phenomena of mental disorder and provide a reformulation of
his research task. Such a task, I have argued, should not be the provision of either mechanistic or conventional, reason-adducing
accounts aimed at covering the whole field of mental disorders or
any specific class or sample of the same. The sociologist must turn
away from 'explanation' of the whys of insanity and toward a

112

description of the hows of insanity *ascription.* The field of inquiry
known as labelling theory, and touched on briefly in a previous discussion, seemed to herald such a reformulation of the sociological
enterprise, but it rapidly degenerated into the provision of docu-
mentary compilations or journalistic exercises in which 'the typical
paths' to a mental hospital were described (sometimes, more rashly,
the 'common properties' of such paths) and frequently such descriptions were used to underpin a quite spurious model of aetiology in
which a man's psychological status was seen as a role adopted
contingently upon his being labelled in a certain way.

Description in sociology, I submit, need not be confined to the
reiteration of disparate members' versions of social processes, nor
to the presentation of journalistic accounts. If so, what is involved
in the sociological description of mental disorders as categories of
social phenomena? Alan Blum has proposed an answer in the following remarks :

> When jurors, psychiatrists, kinsmen, and all ordinary members
> decide the sanity of another, their decisions are ultimately based
> on a socially accredited body of knowledge that they methodically
> use .... The labels (e.g., schizophrenia - JC) which we as
> observers confront are, so to speak, the end points of much socially
> organised activity that enters into their production. To accept
> such end points as points of departure for exploring the antece-
> dent conditions or independent variables that influence the labell-
> ing process ... is to neglect the socially organised character of
> the labelling process itself.[1]

These remarks are informed by the work of Harvey Sacks on the
nature of warrantable sociological description.[2] Sacks, discussing
Durkheim's *Suicide,* noted that any questions about the reasons for
suicide (assuming that there could be *general* answers) presuppose
the warranted assembly of members of the set 'suicided persons' in
the first place. The cultural bases for any assembly of cases of any
social category are investigable. The sociologist can direct his
attention to the description and analysis of the complex cultural
knowledge that informs any warrantable assembly of phenomena
in a society as cases of 'X' (insanity, suicide). Alan Blum, however,
suggests that we display the cultural bases of the work of insanity
ascription in terms of a set of rules, but this is problematic for various
reasons, one of which is that we have already found that professional
psychiatric diagnostic procedures will not succumb to formulation
by rule or algorithm. Moreover, in doing the job of description in

Sacks's terms, we do not need to construe human interaction (including ascriptions) in game-like terms.[3]

Actual ascriptive practices are context-bound and highly variable with respect to the number and relationships of personnel involved, the temporal duration, the manifestations thought of as significant, the actual words spoken, the courses of action taken and other particulars. Analytically, however, insanity ascribing procedures partake of culturally furnished knowledge and belief and presuppose describable sorts of reasoning and inferential work. Instead of seeking to systematise the surface phenomena of actual ascriptions by describing their 'typical' or 'common' factors, the analyst seeks to display the most abstract features of the cultural resources and inferential procedures implicit in or presupposed by any warrantable instance of insanity ascription. Our interest, then, is in a culturally indigenous ethnopsychiatry. Traditionally, however, ethnomethodological work of the sort which Sacks outlines has been concerned with 'what anybody knows,' i.e. commonsense cultural knowledge, and not with epistemic collectivities such as psychiatry. However, there are clear relationships between elements of the 'technical' competence of professional ascribers and ratifiers of ascriptions and the 'untechnical', commonsense competence of ordinary lay members who may make ascriptions. The 'untechnical' competence involved includes knowledge of such cultural items as beliefs, perceptions, motives, speech organisation and so on. We shall have occasion to discuss this in detail as we move on to a consideration of specific forms of ascription. One last point on this. We construe insanity as constituted solely by judgmental processes, by the operation of many culturally specific types of reasoning (and many culturally universal types as well). Nonetheless, judgments of insanity are not always intelligibly subject to doubt, as if there were some suprahuman norm to which we mortals falteringly aspire or as if there are never points at which we are certain, at which doubting must stop on pain of perversity. Sometimes we may warrantably and accountably ascribe insanity on the basis of a one minute discussion with someone along with a chat to relatives or consociates; on other occasions, we may always feel that the person is a borderline case. There is no point in generalising in either direction—either by claiming that insanity ascriptions are human judgments and hence always flawed, or by claiming that all insanity ascriptions are ratified by experts and therefore everyone who is diagnosed insane by professionals *is* unquestionably insane.

Ascriptions of insanity which are often converted or 'scientized' into ascriptions of schizophrenia are pragmatically associated with ascriptions of hallucinatory experiences, disordered thought and delusions. I want to consider each separately, although it is in the nature of the phenomena that we shall encounter overlaps.

SECTION TWO: HALLUCINATIONS

Possessing the faculty of vision (or any other sensory faculty) does not by itself guarantee that one shall be thought of as a conventionally competent perceiver of things and events in the world. In order to pass as a competent member of the seeing community, one must be able to render one's percepts in a conventional way. This involves mastery over a stock of concepts; one could not perceive a table without the concept of 'table', although one could certainly see *something* if one could see at all. Recognition of 'correct' or 'adequate' perception, then, is tied to a recognition of the social distribution of knowledge. Only someone trained in elementary botany could see a stamen; only someone with some knowledge of physiology could see the fibula of a skeleton; only someone with neurophysiological knowledge could see the occipital lobe of a brain; only someone with astronomical knowledge could see the star Cirius in the night sky. When we encounter persons who are able to see things in the universe which we cannot, we can sometimes allocate their ability to command over a specialized body of knowledge and to specific sorts of training. Occasionally, 'theoretic' perceptions which arise out of discriminations and discoveries made by members of epistemic communities such as biology, physics and astronomy, filter into the repertoire of common discriminations and in time may become requisite knowledge for a competent member of the wider collectivity. In a similar sense, other cultures require different sorts of discriminations to be made than the ones which we routinely make; the Eskimos are known to perceive six different types of snow, southern Chinese peasants over ninety different types of rice, and so on. Of course, these peoples do not have to be presumed to have a different sensory apparatus from our own; simply different practical life exigencies and thereby different discriminatory relevances codified into their language.

A member of our own culture who claims to have made a further or a finer discrimination of some range of phenomena for some purpose is expected to be able to teach others (including ourselves were we interested) to perceive his new discriminations. This teaching would naturally involve ostensive techniques coupled to ordinary descriptive protocols. It would be no use for someone simply to announce that he had discerned a *glompf* in the human eye or a *wompit* in a chemical substance or a *curtz* in the Malayan jungles and leave it at that. We should require him to be able to demonstrate the perceptual bases for his new categories or, if possible, to translate them into ordinary descriptive terms. However, if the innovator in question belonged to some class of persons entitled to produce new discoveries or discriminations of things, we may well patiently await the intersubjective corroboration of his finding(s) without ascribing hallucinations to him. Ascriptions of hallucinations, then, cannot simply stem from recognising that someone is seeing or has seen something *unconventional,* since there are categories of competent persons engaged in just such a practice. Thus, we may begin by noting that the social distribution of knowledge and training has an important bearing on the accountability or otherwise of an ascription of hallucinatory experiences.

Perceptual capacities are tied, then, to conceptual capacities and membership categories.[4] We make allowances for conceptual imbalances in certain cases of perceptual imbalances, but we also make allowances for imbalances in types of training and experience. The artist, the craftsman, the skilled electronics engineer each have attributed to them (or could appropriately claim) perceptual abilities of particularly refined types. The experienced musician may be accorded the ability to discriminate finer variations in pitch than the untutored ear; the artist the ability to perceive finer variations in colour tones and textures. However, there is a double sense to the notion of 'conventional'. On the one hand, there is the sense of 'what is now the untechnical, unspecialized, common run' of abilities etc. On the other hand, there is the more restricted sense to which Wittgenstein alluded when he wrote of the conventions of our human forms of life.[5] Some capacity may be unconventional in the first sense but conventional in the second sense; e.g. the artist who can draw a near perfect circle without using a compass or any other artefact than a paintbrush can do something exceptional, extraordinary and unconventional, but the artist who claims that he can see his pictures come to life in the privacy of his studio is claiming something unconventional in the second sense—he is escaping the bounds of credibility of our human forms of life if he makes the claim literally and seriously. We may then have a choice of categorization; extreme eccentricity, deluded belief and/or hallucinations. In the case of a weekend, suburban painter who holds down some other occupation and who claimed the same unconventional percepts, we might be less tempted to consider the escape clause of eccentricity, but this is an area of such indeterminacy that we cannot pursue it very far before getting bogged down in contextual ramifications which need not concern us.

Disjunctions in reported percepts can require explanations. Such explanations may make reference to faulty spectacles, colour-blindness and other contingencies relating to the physical faculties or their technological extensions. Motivated or wilful misperceptions on the part of one or more members may sometimes be found to be the appropriate explanation for discrepancies. We have already looked briefly at the relationship between types of discriminatory perception and the differential distribution of training and/or experience of certain sorts amongst members of a culture, to which the differential distribution of knowledge is closely related : the children in Piaget's famous experiment who perceived the volume of liquid in the tall, thin glass to be more than the amount in the fat, squat glass from which it was poured are imputed to lack the requisite knowledge of conservation relationships and not to suffer from some generalised, infantile sight disorder. Some discrepancies are scored up to hallucinations caused by sensory deprivation, oxygen shortage, lysergic acid or some other hallucinogenic agent, the onset of a neurological condition and so on. Others are attributed to hallucinations which are then used as grounds for inference to insanity. The nature of any discrepancy will obviously inform the nature of permissible accounts for it.

For most mundane discrepancies, members are expected to accede to some conventional explanation, or even to proffer one themselves. They can be found to be joking, lying, stubborn, malicious, argumentative, stupid and the like if they fail to realign their perceptual reports to the available, socially corroborated account(s). Even in the case of hallucinations, the member can be required to deny the authenticity of his percepts and sustain the socially shared definition of reality. A member should not interact with his hallucination(s); he should not incorporate them into a scheme of interpretation unacceptable to consociates; he should not react to consociates by accusing them of inauthentic experience, faulty vision, deafness, inadequate perceptual capacity, malice or conspiracy—in short, he should be able to recognise his hallucinations *as* such once his consociates have firmly agreed that that is what his perceptions amount to. To violate these conventions can be to provide grounds for inferences of insanity. It can involve the loss of membership itself.

In certain cases and for certain groups of people, namely children and religious affiliates, excusing conditions can be found and cited for discrepant perceptions and perceptual claims in which unseen and unheard figures are partners in interaction. For neophytes, adult counter-training should not be resisted continuously, otherwise a psychiatric problem may be suspected and the excusing conditions of linguistic misassimilations, hyper-active imagination and 'reality-testing' might be suspended. For Christian visionaries, mystics, Hindus, Haitian voodoo believers and others, the presence of some degree of social corroboration for their perceptual claims can provide grounds for the eschewal of insanity ascription and even the denial of hallucinations as pathologically present for them.

First person psychological statements about hallucinatory experiences, delivered with appropriate concern for standards of group credibility and conventions of description can form grounds for the sustenance of the attribution of rationality, providing such assertions are not found to have occurred many times earlier in the member's social biography, and they may even prompt tentative observers' reformulations of the perceptions (e.g. the person may not be thought to have hallucinated, only to have misinterpreted some perfectly real phenomenon). The point here is that the member gives no indication that his thinking or his system of beliefs are at fault, even though there may be some issue to be raised about his problematic perception. If such a first person psychological assertion is biographically *isolated* from the rest of the member's functioning, and if he seems prepared to seek help himself, then a physical rather than a purely mental dysfunction might be suspected.

For those members whose hallucinations are counted as grounds for the ascription of insanity (or, more generally, 'schizophrenia'), first person assertions of rational sorts are absent. The hallucinations are inferred from the member's statements of *belief* about certain things, or from his incongruous conduct in the presence of others which involves reacting to unseen and unheard presences. It is assumed that one can be deluded *about* one's hallucinations or deluded *because* of them. The incorporation of hallucinatory experiences into delusional systems is often thought to arise because of the member's isolation from reality-sustaining and deviance-ascribing others in the community. Moreover, deluded beliefs have perceptual implications or bases (such as the belief in the malice of next door neighbours who scream at the member all night long, or a persecution belief involving reference to cloaked and hooded figures who constantly pursue him).

A claim about a drug free, hallucinatory experience, then, does not automatically engender the ascription of mental disorder. Reference must always be made to other contingencies which complicate the picture, and I have suggested what some of these might look like. A recurrent issue in ascriptions of schizophrenia is the status of the member as a commonsense theorizer. The competence, or adequacy, of one's *thinking* is at the core of the matter. Indeed, the status of a member's thinking about his perceptions informs the utility or otherwise of arguments and checking procedures (wherever logically possible) with respect to his troubles. (Mental health personnel naturally differ with respect to their evaluations of the usefulness of argument and checks for particular cases, but it is clear that the limits to such are given in the member's apparent ability to respect rational canons of argument and demonstration.) For example, in the case of a man referred to a large mental health department by the police for having been found huddled and naked in the street and muttering about a Spanish galleon having crashed in through his front window, there seemed little point to anyone in arguing with him about the impossibility of such an occurrence, or even the chance that he misconstrued some perfectly real event. On the other hand, one conflict arose between officers' accounts and handling of a situation in which an elderly lady, living alone, was involved. She was reported by one officer as deluded in that she believed she was being persecuted by her next door neighbours, and she had been referred by her general practitioner on the grounds that she was in 'poor mental health'. She believed that her neighbours were projecting light beams on her windows all night long and sending violent electric shocks through her limbs by wiring up the house with live wires, coupled to which she complained of hearing their threats whilst in bed, along with the noises of a 'workshop'. These 'interferences', as she called them, were written up as auditory hallucinations and delusions. Another officer, taking up the home visits to this client, noted that she occupied a house on a busy street connecting with an arterial route through the city, that her sitting-room and bedroom windows all faced the street, with no pavement between her house and the street itself. The walls separating her house from next door were thin and crumbling, and talking could easily be heard from there. Further, the woman was suffering from an acute arthritic condition. There were the elements of a rational accounting scheme for each element of the client's hallucinations and delusions. The light beams were traffic headlights at night, and the workshop noises were traffic noises. The electric shocks were arthritic pains. The voices were indeed from her neighbours (though not necessarily threatening). On this basis, the new officer (to the case, not to the job) decided to attempt a transformation of the woman's definitions of her situation by encouragement, argument and persuasion, and eventually created a new relationship between her and the next door neighbours. The recurrence of complaints on her part about them dissipated and her delusions abated, at least temporarily. Not all such attempts seem to succeed, but the point is that for some members the attempt is seen to be worth a try. More-over, no arguments can even be considered unless there are *some* possibilities of rational decipherment to be proposed to the member in question or to serve as the basis for therapeutic reorientation of the member's conduct and belief. No officer expects to be able to dissipate someone's hallucinations simply by counter-assertion or by a blatant insistence upon standards of perceptual propriety. Such tactics are fit only for suspected fakers or frauds.

I want to turn to deal with a recorded interchange between a mental welfare officer and a man living in the community referred to the mental health department by his flatmate because of his moodiness, irritability and refusal to get out of bed, day after day—a condition which arose shortly after the man's brother's death.

*MWO:* How long is't since yer brother died, Frank?
*Frank:* About a year.
                    (Pause)
*MWO:* D'ya . . . think . . . about 'im much?

*Frank:* Yeah. (Pause) Quite a bit.

*MWO:* Errm ... d'ya ever hear him? In yer thoughts I mean. D'ya ever hear his voice?

*Frank:* No. (Pause) No. I think about 'im.

*MWO:* Are they yer own thoughts or yer brother's, Frank?

(Pause)

*Frank:* Me own thoughts ....

*MWO:* Does yer brother ... er ... yer brother ever speak t'ya from beyond?

(Pause)

*Frank:* They're me own thoughts ....


The officer's line of questioning is informed by the fragmentary biographical data incorporated into the referral agent's report to the mental health department; officers necessarily operate with such data as contextual supplementation for some of the questions they ask and for providing schemes of interpretation for relevant answers (i.e. answers which are informative about the subject's psychological state). Having determined that the man Frank still thought 'quite a bit' about his dead brother, the officer could proceed on that issue and he does so by enquiring about the nature of the thoughts themselves. Given limited time and resources, mental health personnel must do an ad hoc operation of probing where they think necessary in order to obtain grounds for inference to psychological status; it is not always possible to allow mundane conversation to develop in the hope that it might generate such grounds by itself, and officers frequently force the issue in an attempt to detect any undisplayed mental problems. In terms of the presuppositions of such a strategy, one might observe that its use is not deterred by preliminary negative responses which might, after all, be further evidence of the covertness of the 'real, underlying' trouble, or the result of disorientation in the face of direct challenge. Moreover, the challenge to a possibly covert hallucinator is not simply one involving the term 'hallucination'—presumably, a man who does not avow such an experience might have constructed a delusional stystem around it by failing to acknowledge its unreality. The officer in the above interchange could be understood as employing an ad hoc diagnostic procedure which informed his questioning : the link between the brother's death and the gross lethargy and irritability might suggest more than depression, and a covert psychotic state cannot be ruled out without some attempt to test that hunch. If these remarks are warrantable, then we can see in the above interchange several aspects of the work of psychiatric reasoning. However, there is another side to this. If we leave aside any consideration of who was speaking to whom, where and why, and treat the transcribed talk in isolation from such detail, then we can read into it quite different contextual possibilities. We could treat it as a conversation between a bereaved man and a believer in the supernatural, perhaps a spiritualist. In fact, the co-conversationalists must themselves employ background knowledge of their respective socially sanctioned categorisations in order to align their discourse appropriately to one another. Speaking under the auspices of his membership of a mental health department making an inquiry, the officer's contribution is restricted to interrogatives which could appear quite in place were he speaking as a ghost-hunter or inquisitive spiritualist. If his interrogatives are to be taken by his co-conversationalist as legitimate elements in psychiatric interview, then the interlocutor must orient to the occasion in that way, and that involves recognizing the authority of the visiting officer to establish such an occasion of talk. The 'occasion' is not explicitly bounded by announcement of start and termination, but does seem conventionally to be initiated by the officer unilaterally with the interlocutor restricting himself to the role of a *participant-object*. This means delivering outward displays of inner thoughts, feelings, beliefs and so on. What gets said can, wherever possible, be read for its 'underlying' significance, for its betrayal of unarticulated problems, *notwithstanding* any peremptory attempts at terminating the line of questioning by the interlocutor. There is, of course, the possibility that a referred person might treat the officer's interrogatives as *illegitimate* elements in the attempt to establish a psychiatrically-motivated occasion of talk, i.e. as irrelevant to what is bothering him, or he might refuse to allow any such occasion to get off the ground by showing the officer to the door or treating his questions as *other than* those informed by his membership category (in the above interchange, that would perhaps have taken the form of a counter-challenge to the officer, e.g.: 'Who are you, some kind of spiritualist?'). As one mental welfare officer told me, if a referred person is willing to 'talk', then the chance that something may be the matter cannot be left unchecked.

Mental welfare officers at all levels operate with the concept of 'insight'. This means a recognition on the part of a patient that he or she is ill and requires help; in other words, the acceptance of a psychiatric definition of one's situation. It is a kind of 'middle ground' between rationality and unmitigated madness. Understanding how it is used in the case of hallucinations helps to reveal aspects of the knowledge and assumptions operable in mental welfare dealings with community clients. I have already noted that first person avowals of hallucinatory experiences can be distinguished from assertions of belief from which a hallucinatory condition can be inferred, and I have drawn attention to the attempts that have been made to reorient a person's conduct on the grounds that the ascription of hallucinations might conceivably have been too hasty or that some other account for the person's beliefs might be feasible. Of course, there are many cases where discussion and argument with the particular person are ruled out as useless, at least for the present. One officer put it this way :

> ... sometimes it's possible to get them [patients in the community] to gain insight into the fact that these *are* hallucinations; it is possible to persuade some people to believe you about this, and it's this combined social work cum medical support that will maintain them in the community.

The judicious use of drugs coupled to persistent social work visits can sometimes combine to enable a person to disentangle his sense dependent percepts from real world perception, and this involves getting him to suspend his own delusional belief system in which he has incorporated his perceptions and to put his trust in, to believe in, the version offered by the mental welfare authorities. This may not guarantee the reassessment of his psychological status as 'sane', but may well enable him to keep out of the mental hospital.

SECTION THREE : DISORDERED THOUGHT

Clinicians and mental welfare agents sometimes have to deal with members of the community whose speech is recognised to betray inadequate thought processes. Indeed, the notions of 'thought disorder' and 'schizophrenic language' (or 'schizophrenic speech' or 'logic') are found to be interchangeable for them. Since the person manifesting disordered thought appears to believe that he is talking sense, that he is communicating intelligibly and sustaining a reciprocity in interaction, he is hardly expected to be in a position to avow his own thought disorder. Unlike hallucinations, thought disorder cannot be avowed in first person psychological assertions and is only and exclusively ascribed to members by others.

It is clear enough that all cases of warrantable insanity ascription involve the ascription of cognitive disorder. We have noted that hallucinations are bound up with delusional interpretive systems where 'schizophrenia' is invoked, and harbouring a delusional system (or simply a preoccupying delusion) signifies that something is wrong with one's thinking about things. Grossly inappropriate conduct, bizarre gesturing, catatonic withdrawal and other indexically identifiable and groundless deviances are also attributable to dysfunctions in one's thinking. However, the category of thought disorder is restricted in application by theoreticians to linguistic peculiarities at the formal levels of syntactic disarray, semantic disorder and discrepancies in sequential organisation in utterances and between utterances where someone else is speaking to the subject. Attempts to draw up a list of the formal characteristics of 'schizophrenic communication' have been made on many occasions throughout the history of psychopathology. William Alanson White's famous paper 'The Language of Schizophrenia'[6] was one of the first to approach the subject with a systematizing inclination, and C. J. Raven, writing in 1958,[7] proposed the following set of discriminations on the basis of research on thought-disordered patients : disordered syntax, obsessional repetition ('perseveration'), bizarre content (semantic peculiarities), rigidity of expression, poverty of expression, circumstantial talk (sic), structural vagueness, distractedness, chain associations, telescoping of ideational content, nonsense words, dissipated and echo responses, excessive stylization and negativistic response tendencies. It is obvious that all of these descriptions could be used to categorise spoken and written productions of ordinary people on diverse occasions, and a string of them might easily be found appended to a badly written school essay. Indeed, generalized descriptions are quite useless if they are proposed as explicit recognition rules for communicative styles peculiar (or 'pathognomic') to thought disorder in schizophrenia. We have wide tolerances in everyday discourse for what we are prepared to accept as appropriate and intelligible speech, and the sort of pejorative epithets which we use to castigate ungrammatical and meaningless utterances on the part of people whom we consider quite sane are no different from those we use when evaluating the communicative conduct of someone whom we are prepared to consider mad or schizophrenic. This does not *vitiate* our evaluations in the latter case, but it does mean that we are without definitive terms for the abstract portrayal of those features of thought-disordered communication which justify that particular designation. Theorists who have sought to specify exactly the constituents of 'schizophrenese' (sometimes resorting to quantitative descriptions such as verb frequencies and adjective distributions) forget that there is no necessary relationship between describable regularities in syntactic and semantic organisation and the pragmatic grounds on which any particular ascription gets made. Further, Lorenz has warned against generalizing from a few regularities (some of which are discernible only through the mediation of statistical sorting) in samples of language used by diagnosed schizophrenics to the existence of *a* 'schizophrenic language'.[8] To ask for a 'schizophrenic dictionary' and a 'schizophrenic grammar' for use in lay and professional diagnostics is as senseless as asking for a 'poetic dictionary' and 'poetic grammar' which must be consulted in the making of any decision about whether or not someone is reciting poetry or becoming a poet. Research whose aim is to test levels of psychiatric agreement as to the degree of 'schizophrenicity' exhibited by samples of speech (such as the work of Hunt and Arnoff)[9] perpetuates the illusion that there is some isolable and determinate phenomenon of schizophrenic language, to whose distinctive properties clinicians are somehow mysteriously responsive. The mania for operationalization in this area attained its zenith in the following remarks by Harold J. Vetter :

At clinical staff meetings, as the present writer can affirm from direct experience, it is by no means unusual to hear statements to the effect that a particular patient 'sounded schizophrenic'. When asked to define the 'schizophrenic sound,' the clinician may react in one of several ways. He may dismiss the question and the questioner; he may tell the questioner that it is difficult to describe exactly what the 'schizophrenic sound' is, but that any experienced psychologist or psychiatrist knows what he means; or he may honestly admit that he is unable to delineate the expression more accurately. It is in this respect that the potential significance of acoustic analysis and sound spectography becomes apparent for psychiatry. By means of techniques such as these, we may eventually be able to operationalise the 'schizophrenic sounds' to the extent that we can add another reliable instrument to our diagnostic collection.[10]

The prospect of ascribing or ratifying schizophrenia to someone on *phonemic* grounds would be alarming were it not comic, and one might enquire about the contents of the diagnostic collection of reliable 'instruments' which psychiatrists are supposed to wield these days. Psychopathologists are so often theoretically disengaged from the routine, commonsense practices of insanity ascription that they risk such mammoth conceptual blundering. Abstract accounts of thought-disordered communication underpinning theoretical speculation are quite idle in the sense that they are disengaged from the interactional locations and settings in which the label is found applicable.

The idea that those verbal productions of persons clinically assessed as thought-disordered derive from some fundamental, isolatable defect in logical reasoning ability was suggested by Von Domarus in a paper entitled 'The Specific Laws of Logic in Schizophrenia'.[11] His experience of patients in the insane asylum of the University of Bonn prompted his conceptualization of the 'core process' involved in schizophrenic speech as a flaw in logical reasoning, and in particular one patient seemed to him to exemplify quite starkly his notion of 'paralogic'. This patient, diagnosed as a schizophrenic, believed that Jesus, cigar boxes and sex were identical phenomena. (We are not told explicitly how such a belief or belief-system was attributed to the patient, whether by inference from conduct, by first person avowals, or by inference from his talk about these things). When some reason for this identification of such disparate phenomena as the same was sought out, one connection was apparently 'discovered'. (Again, we are not told how). This was that all three phenomena were 'encircled' : Jesus by a halo, cigar boxes by their tax bands and women by the sexual glance of men. (This latter is obviously disjunctive in that the sexual glance or, for the patient, sex itself, is not encircled by a halo—it *constitutes* the halo in some sense. This anomaly makes it imperative that we ascertain how the connection was discovered and by whom, but our needs are left unsatisfied.) Von Domarus suggested that this paralogical identification of disparate phenomena might underlie and inform the entire process of disordered thought, reasoning and communication in some pathognomic manner (he considered his theory to state the *specific* laws of logic in schizophrenia). He wrote :

... whereas the logician accepts identity only upon the basis of identical subjects, the paralogician accepts identity based upon identical predicates.[12]

Let us first dispense with 'laws' of logic (a throwback to the early philosophies in which the 'laws' of logic were identified with the equally puzzling 'laws of thought') and speak instead of 'rules' of logic. In doing this we make obvious provision for such occurrences as violations, defiances and infractions of the rules (one cannot violate a law). Further, let us consider the nature of some ordinary deductive procedures. We can imagine someone who knew that oak trees were deciduous encountering a tree and being unable to classify it for some purpose. Then he hits on the idea of asking a nearby resident if he has ever noticed whether that particular tree sheds its leaves all together or not, and he is informed that it does. From this he can assume, with some rationality, that the new tree in question is an oak tree, although he would be stupid to be fully satisfied with that very simple deduction. Nonetheless, he has (perhaps only provisionally) accepted identity on the basis of identical predicates. Let us suppose that he has accepted the identity of this tree with oak trees, about which he has read and seen various (indecisive) drawings and photographs, on the basis of identical predicates, and he has accepted that identity wholeheartedly. We might be tempted to call him rash, deride his lack of thoroughness and so on if we found out that he required more accurate knowledge for purposes of locating a setting for a film in which the script demanded that the surrounding trees were oaks, but we would probably not feel inclined to berate him if there was no such pressing purpose informing his classificatory quest.

Von Domarus's formulation, then, is too vague to do the job he wants it to do. He has focused on one fraction of the pattern of mundane human reasoning and omitted considerations about routine deductive procedures which are carried out in the form he ascribes exclusively to the reasoning of thought-disordered persons. There are clearly other possibilities for the interpretation of the case of the Bonn patient, which have nothing to do with the more general capacity for constructing syllogisms. One of these is that the patient may have been obsessively thematically preoccupied; another is that, since his peculiarity consisted in accepting identity on the basis of a very *odd* predicate for the phenomena, he may have been using a delusional classification system which might itself have been very restricted in scope for him. We cannot know for sure what sort of reasoning *was* used (if indeed there was any at all), since any premises remained tacit (which is also the case for common-sense, enthymematic arguments carried on by perfectly rational people). Von Domarus' theory seems to me to be yet another instance of the failure to distinguish between conduct which *accords* with some stipulated rule, and conduct which is the *application* of some rule by the agent. The speech and conduct of schizophrenics, no matter how diverse they may be, can always be brought under the jurisdiction of some set of rules we may wish to formulate, but we cannot proceed from there to ascribe our rules to the patients themselves, as if they are using *our* rules (or *any* rules) to produce *their* conduct. In summary, then, since no isolable logical defect can adequately characterise those cases and only those cases to which the label 'thought-disordered' is warrantably attached, then we cannot use such a characterisation to guide our ascriptive work as lay and professional members arriving at practical decisions.

The category of 'thought-disorder' is quasi-technical, unlike the categories of 'hallucination' and 'delusion'. Its use by psychiatrists and mental health officials is to be expected, but not normally by lay members. Inasmuch as this is the case, the category can be used in such a way as to suggest to the uninitiated, lay psychological theoriser (the rest of us) that it denotes some underlying state of affairs which *explains* the deviant modes of communication recognised in certain persons, in a manner analogous to the use of the category 'paresis' in organic psychiatry. Instead of realising that the category use frequently amounts to an 'appraisal', members can be led to believe that it amounts to an 'explanation'. The disordered talk arises *because of* the thought disorder, instead of expressing it. This version makes it possible for professionals to argue that people can be thought-disordered in covert ways, and that it can be *elicited* by judicious questioning or some other interpersonal strategy, since it is a 'condition' existing separately from people's speaking practices even though it can only be revealed through such practices. In other words, people can be thought to suffer from 'thought disorder' even on occasions where they are speaking normally; the underlying state of disordered thought can be externalized by the psychiatrist or mental health official (often through confronting someone with a supposedly well known proverb and requiring the person to complete it). This assumption that thought disorder is a continuous state with discontinuous manifestations informs the denials by mental health officials that persons referred, who are reported as having at some time spoken in a disjointed and peculiar way for no apparent reason, are undergoing a quite *episodic* experience. The other assumption, that thought disorder is an intermittently recurrent state (and thus cannot be 'elicited'), still gets used to warrant the treatment of persons so reported as candidates for the ascription of disordered thought—once such a report is made and authenticated (e.g. by reference to the status of referral agent, by corroborations, etc.), then the person involved cannot normally escape psychiatric probing even when he speaks rationally in the presence of a mental health official, and where the official would concur that his speech was orderly.

Psychopathologists have, in their various ways, attempted to formulate some general basis for the 'condition' of disordered thought whilst ignoring the sort of issues which are raised from the actual conduct of psychiatric ascriptive and investigative practices concerning this category. Psychiatrists, however, because their assumptions differ with respect to its use, do not present us with a homogeneous picture of disordered thought, and they entertain no general theory about it in the conduct of their work. Instead, since their ascriptions (and elicitations) are ad hoc, so also are their ideas about causation (wherever they articulate such ideas). The following piece of data will help to clarify this:

MWO: (reporting on a case history to a psychiatric social worker) ... A few days later, errm ... his behaviour was described as erratic and disturbing to the family ... errm ... the GP, the psychiatrist are on record as having visited ... errm ... and he [the patient] was said to be very guarded, but when pressed ... errm ... thought disorder was elicited. Errm ... I think, you know, again this is interesting that he was thought to be under pressure again when these symptoms were—came out, you know, errm ... he went on, on that occasion, into hospital, and ...

PSW: Did they describe the thought disorder?

MWO: No.

PSW: They did say it was thought disorder but they don't say what it was.

The ad hoc connection between 'pressure' and disordered thought, which is reported here, arose also in a case where a woman who was referred as suicidal failed to 'converse consistently' and failed a proverb test. The psychiatrist who was making the domiciliary visit suggested to the mental welfare officer that her thought-disordered state was the result of frustrated suicidal drives and living under pressure. Other ad hoc connections found include lack of sleep caused by worry, nervous exhaustion and senility. The use of a situated rationale does not imply the use of a situated justification because the two are distinguished by mental health agents. Someone can be thought-disordered and their sanity brought into serious question even when some context specific basis for it is identified and articulated, since for the purposes of ad hoc theorizing such a 'basis' might only be a tenuous one in which the phenomenon (thought disorder in this case) is assimilated into a class of phenomena for which one *can* cite anxiety, worry and so forth as reasons. This attenuating assimilation is frequently used by mental health agents in the presence of kin as a kind of technique of reassurance, since if the symptom(s) are seen as more or less equivalent to the sorts of troubles for which social pressures and the like can be cited as reasons, then there is at least the hope that social work and medical care can induce a transformation in the person affected. Many psychiatrists find the category of 'functional mental disorders' useful in the sense that it enables them warrantably to propose that, for some cases, social work support and remedial psychotherapeutic regimes can counteract the symptoms since these are after all only extreme expressions of emotional disorganization which we all experience (or can envisage) as within the range of ordinary living. If a total disjunction from such a range is proposed for a particular case and this is communicated to kin, then this can seriously undermine parents' or spouses' confidence in the ability of psychiatry to remedy the situation. Dr E. F. Kal expressed some of the dilemmas faced by some psychiatrists which arise from the uncertainties surrounding the organic/functional dichotomy in the following way :

> Does the clinician label a condition organic in order to absolve himself from blame if he fails to cure it—or because he dislikes the patient and doesn't want to bother with psychotherapy—or because prescribing medication gives him a sense of control which the nebulousness of psychogenicity does not provide him with? Or does he prefer a psychological and social aetiologic explanation because admitting an organic defect would leave him much too

hopeless—or again because he can criticize and confront the schizophrenigenic mother?'[13]

Psychiatrists have a choice in characterizing persons who manifest disordered thought. Either they can perpetuate the category mistake of psychopathology and construe it as a 'symptom' of some other underlying mental state called 'schizophrenia' (in the sense in which jaundice is understood as the 'symptom' of infectious hepatitis or bile-duct blockage).'[14] or they can construe it as constitutive of 'schizophrenia' and thereby deny any antecedent or independent status to the latter. This choice is often settled by reference to one's theoretical preference; if one favours an organic account of 'schizophrenia', then one will probably opt for the former characterisation which accords independent disease status to it, whereas if one opts for a functional view, one is free to consider the concept 'schizophrenia' to consist in no more and no less than the presentations of subjects so diagnosed. Such a choice is generally restricted to case conferences and inter-psychiatric discussion of cases. It can, however, become an issue for interested parties in some committal decision since the assimilation of their friend's condition to conditions of physical illness is one method of removing him from moral stigmatization, whilst the 'functional' alternative leaves the matter ambiguous with respect to considerations of moral responsibility and causation.

SECTION FOUR: DELUSIONS

Any community of communicators is a community of co-believers; without some shared beliefs, no orderly communication between people can proceed. As Wittgenstein pointed out, many of our factual beliefs constitute the 'unmoving' foundations of our language games,[15] and form the conventional infrastructure for so many of our assertions, enquiries, experiences, tests and certainties. These intersubjective, foundational beliefs are not all intelligibly subject to doubt, even though we may find it difficult 'to realise the groundlessness of our believing'[16] that certain things are the case. Since any testing presupposes *some* untested believing, and since learning cannot all be accomplished through testing for oneself, 'doubt comes *after* belief'.[17] We learn our natural language and factual beliefs pari passu, and together with that we find the socially sanctified areas of *legitimate* doubting. Wittgenstein remarked :

> There are cases such that, if someone gives signs of doubt where we do not doubt, we cannot confidently understand his signs as signs of doubt.
> I.e. : if we are to understand his signs of doubt as such, he may give them only in particular cases and may not give them in others.[18]

If we are in a position where we find someone apparently 'doubting' something which we find (and claim others would also find) no grounds for doubting (e.g., the existence of hands at the end of his arms), then we may treat such 'signs of doubt' as 'signs of defect'—the apparent doubter is not after all doubting, but is stupid, joking, pretending or insane.

> If someone said to me that he doubted whether he had a body I should take him to be a half-wit. But I shouldn't know what it would mean to try to convince him that he had one. And if I had said something, and that had removed his doubt, I should not know how or why.[19]

Collective authority establishes the credentials for beliefs. This is also true of knowledge : 'Knowledge is in the end based on acknowledgement,'[20] as Wittgenstein put it. Belief claims are frequently 'guarded declaratives'. Knowledge claims are unguarded declaratives. If I utter an unguarded declarative and am proved wrong, then I will reassess my prior claim as a 'belief claim' : it would be odd for me to say, 'I knew X then, but now I know not-X (or Y).' It is this regularity in retrospective 'guarding' which enables us to find it funny when we read that the Pope, in pronouncing a change in an infallible assertion, has merely moved 'from one state of certainty to another'. We would normally render our former claim as a belief claim and our present claim as a knowledge claim, but infallibilists are not permitted the luxury of guarded declaratives.

When we pronounce on the claims of others about things in the world, we often exercise our third person declaratives in a guarded way (by saying e.g. 'He believes that P.'), even though the ones we are talking about are making knowledge claims. This is strikingly evident in the transcultural literature. When writing about the Azande oracles and witchcraft, many anthropologists write of 'Azande *belief* in witchcraft', or the 'Azande *belief* in the powers of the oracle,' whilst drawing ironic contrasts with 'Western scientific *knowledge*'.[21] In ascribing beliefs to people where they would affirm knowledge, we are expressing reservations about their knowledge claims. Within our community, scientifically validated propositions about the world constitute a part of our socially accredited body of knowledge, and if anyone articulates any of these propositions he does not need to preface his assertions with 'I believe that . . .' unless he wishes to appear modest or undogmatic.

> Supposing we met people who did not regard [a proposition of physics] as a telling reason [for some action e.g. taking precautions about boiling water or insulating one's pipes against the frost]. Now, how do we imagine this? Instead of the physicist, they consult an oracle. (And for that we consider them primitive.) Is it wrong for them to consult an oracle and be guided by it?—If we call this 'wrong' aren't we using our language game as a base from which to *combat* theirs? . . .
> At the end of reasons comes *persuasion.* (Think what happens when missionaries convert natives.)[22]

It makes sense to seek to *persuade* someone whose factual claims and everyday practices are denied the bestowal of knowledge status and objective adequacy; the first step in undermining someone's version of the world or of things that happen in that world is to deprive it of the status of knowledge and to construe it as mere belief. In Wittgenstein's example of the missionaries, however, something rather odd occurs—the missionaries speak of substituting *belief* in God for belief in witchcraft, not of substituting *knowledge* of God for belief in witchcraft. Sometimes they will express themselves rhetorically by claiming that they are instilling into the natives a *knowledge* of the One True God, but if pressed they will be content to assert (usually) that theirs is a *belief* sustained by faith, or that they are certain in their *belief.* In this, they are acceding to a convention which seems tacitly to accept as a paradigm for knowledge something like the sort of propositions which natural scientists produce when doing science, against which they measure their own factual claims (e.g. the existence of God, the Resurrection, the miracles etc) and find them candidates for the status of belief rather than knowledge. It seems to me that whilst cross cultural comparisons of supernatural beliefs is reasonable, comparisons of the supernatural beliefs of one culture with the corpus of knowledge generated by scientific institutions in another culture is quite ridiculous if it results in construing the former as a poor cousin of the latter. (This appears to be the position of some philosophers of social science, notably Jarvie and Gellner, who seem to think that it is the business of anthropologists to be 'uncharitable' to some of the metaphysical claims which underpin many of the everyday activities of some small African and Asian tribes.)

The attempt to substitute what we consider to be aberrant or irrational beliefs with hard, socially corroborated knowledge can be found within a culture where some of its members articulate factual claims which we find peculiar and unsupportable. In certain circumstances, we refer to these aberrant claims as *delusions*. Quite often, the attempt to dissipate a delusion or 'delusional system' will not involve the provision of arguments purporting to *prove* that something else is the case. Instead, such an attempt may feature remarks which assume that the person 'really knows better' than to believe that *p*, or may make reference to the socially unsupported character of the claims in question (e.g. 'No-one's going to believe you if you tell them that . . .' 'You do realise that you're on your own in believing that, don't you?' or 'If I were you, I'd keep that idea to myself'), or to the instrumentally deleterious consequences that can be evisaged to follow from sustaining (or acting on the basis of) such claims (e.g. 'O.K., O.K., you believe that if you want to—but you'll soon find you've no friends left if you keep on insisting that they're all out to kill you,' 'I can't prove that you're wrong, but you'll get your life into a mess if you persist in that line of thinking . . .' or 'If your landlord finds out that you think the other tenants are using ray-guns against you, *you'll* be the one to get evicted, not them,' etc). In fact, as we have already noted from Wittgenstein's discussion of reasonable belief and reasonable doubt, there are some beliefs (and some doubts of mundane beliefs) for which we can find nothing to say in terms of concrete correctives. Sometimes, we feel it a waste of time even to discuss with a problematic believer :

> It is quite sure that motor cars don't grow out of the earth. We feel that if someone could believe the contrary he could believe *everything* that we say is untrue, and could question everything that we hold to be sure . . . . We should like to say that someone who could believe that does not accept our whole system of verification.[23]

We can say '*it* is quite sure that . . .' and '*it* is certain that . . .' in such a 'neutral' way because in so doing we are appealing to collective authority, to socially accepted and enforced standards of credibility and evidence, of justification and 'sufficient grounds'. But this does not mean that the collective authority lies beyond ourselves, with our role like that of a passive conveyer of its edicts and principles. We constantly construct, affirm and enforce a collective authority *intersubjectively*. This anthropocentrism is expressed in the phrase : '*our* whole system of verification'. We sustain it; it does not sustain itself *through* us. But we cannot drop it at will and adopt something else in its place. It is humanly constructed and therefore conventional, but not arbitrary (any more than our 'humanness' could be said to be arbitrary). When one of us does appear to jettison that system by believing something which we find wholly untenable, either because there are no grounds that could make sense to us *as* grounds for that belief, or because one cannot believe that on *those* grounds, or because there are reasonable, or 'good enough' grounds for believing the contrary, then we confront the possibility of tolerating more than one system of verification, of adequacy criteria, or of sustaining ours to the detriment of the other. Quite often, in sustaining our own, we are driven to say : 'This is how we think and speak,' and sometimes we feel that this is a precarious sort of 'ultimate justification,' even though it is the only logically possible one.

Our system of verification includes verification by reference to established authorities who are entitled to know, to textbooks, to what is repeatedly experienced, to what is heard, to controlled and uncontrolled observation, to test, to experiment and so on, depending upon what is available. There are limits to the lengths to which we are prepared (or required) to go before we accept certain propositions as established knowledge, beyond which we travel on pain of pedantry and, ultimately, unintelligibility. It is verified for me that a particle of light travels at 186,000 miles per second by my having read it in a physics text recommended to me by someone whose judgement I respect in these matters; I have no idea of how to go about verifying such information myself, and no idea about the measurement operations used to determine such facts. Similarly, I know that the existence of Australia is massively verified for me through films, books, people's tales and so on without my ever having been there myself; I also know that X is my brother without ever having set eyes on his birth certificate because that fact has been verified for me by my having been brought up with him in the same family unit to treat him *as* my brother, and it would take some very potent arguments to engender doubts about that. Some people seriously espouse beliefs which do not fall into the category of legitimate, socially supported superstition or religion, but rather into the category of bizarre idiosyncracy. These people, whether they believe that they are God, a machine, a corpse, or a many-headed hydra, appear to us to operate quite outside the bounds of our system of verification and are therefore candidates for the ascription of insanity. Moreover, since they seem oblivious to our standards of inference and evidence then we find difficulty in making commonsense predictions about their conduct and in so organizing our communication with them that we avoid reinforcing their deviant belief(s). People with 'ideas of reference' are especially and notoriously troublesome in this respect: they believe that interactants are covertly making fun of them or otherwise degrading their social status etc, and if one is seeking to establish some kind of therapeutic or social work relationship with them one must attend to one's presentation of oneself with great caution, lest they detect *further* evidence of furtive mockery or even conspiratorial probing. People with irrational persecution beliefs are found to build up their (often internally coherent) world picture from such tiny fragments of talk and appearance, and by attaching great significance to such passing incidents in their lives, that anyone attempting to establish a relationship with them is faced with the problem of having to avoid amiguities and references which might be treated by such people as corroborations of their paranoid constructions. One often hears mental welfare officers talking of 'unwittingly adding fuel to the fire' in cases of ideas of reference and persecution. Their perennial problem lies in being unable to tell in advance just what sort of references and remarks could be construed in a deleterious sense.

As Wittgenstein noted, if someone believes that $p$, and $p$ is something that goes against our fundamental conventions of mundane life, then we could expect him to believe anything which we could not. This underlies the notion of delusional incorporation which is used by some mental health officials as an organising principle for doing social work with deluded people. It is held that if mundane artefacts or next door neighbours are being construed as malevolent or menacing by certain people, then such people are quite likely to perceive and interpret an innocent visit by a local authority agent, a relative or the milkman within their deluded scheme, or to treat more and more domestic objects as sources of evil (my tape-recorded was singled out on more than one occasion as an object liable to be thought malevolent by certain patients with machine delusions, even though tape-recorders had not hitherto featured in their considerations). Occasionally some attempt at 'neutralization' of my recorder was made.

*Mother of patient living at home:* I just told you . . . you know what a tape-recorder is, don't you?
*Patient:* Mm.
*Mother:* Eh? . . . That's all it is . . .
*MWO:* Just like your radio, Sheila, when you switch your radio on that's what it's like.
*Patient:* Mm.
*MWO:* You can hear voices it doesn't do you anything does it when it comes on the wireless?
*Patient:* Yeah . . . mm.
*MWO:* Well, that's the same thing only that's a little box instead.

When a mental health official tries to argue with a patient (something that happens rarely) in order to try to dissipate his delusions, he very often finds himself the victim of the patient's closed system of thinking. On one occasion, a mental welfare officer was trying to dissuade a woman from believing that she was a television camera broadcasting her thoughts to the TV sets of the entire city. She suggested that she could prove that she was right by switching on her own TV set. Having done this, the two of them (MWO and patient) noted that the TV was showing the test-card, and the woman triumphantly declared that it was precisely that which she was thinking about. Again, one man who believed that his eyeballs had become fixed in a frontal gaze in his sockets tried to prove it by getting the officer to look with him into a mirror! Sometimes, a patient will listen carefully to everything that the officer has said by way of arguments against his beliefs, and will then remark : 'Well look, I'll explain more . . .,' proceeding to reiterate the delusion yet again, perhaps accompanying this second account with disclaimers such as : '*They'll* think I'm deluded, but . . .' Many patients account for counter-arguments by invoking secondary elaborations of their initial beliefs, whilst others simply claim that although the counter-argument has some point it will not suffice when weighed against everything else (much of which, of course, is not open to check or test by anyone). Delusions are the result of the application of a bizarre judgemental procedure, and what has to be learnt is not some fresh set of beliefs but a different *style of judgement* if the delusions are to be dissipated.

It is often noted that many people are known to believe bizarre and unusual things without becoming candidates for insanity ascription. Sometimes, it is argued, such people are 'suffering' from 'mild forms' of paranoia or other category of mental disorder, but since their lives are not unduly disorganized by a preoccupation with their beliefs, and since they do not appear to constitute any threat or danger to others, they escape the attention of agents of psychiatric control. This fact informs the argument for a 'continuum' theory of mental disorders generally, in which ordinary styles of conduct are seen to merge into abnormal and ultimately psychotic styles by degree. As a general perspective on insanity, this is quite wide of the mark. I have made reference earlier in this work to the qualitative break from conventional, normatively ordered conduct involved in warrantably assessed cases of insanity, and Rimland has argued powerfully against the misplaced humanitarianism of the theory of insanity as 'unhappiness magnified'.[24] This is not to deny for one moment that we routinely use the same set of evaluative descriptors applied to psychotic conduct in application to conduct which we do not consider insane in its own contexts. We talk about some religious and/or political beliefs with which we profoundly disagree as 'weird', 'mad', 'crazy', 'bizarre' and 'utterly senseless,' etc, and we even make reference to each other's everyday conduct in such terms on occasion without any reference to a psychiatrist nor any undertones of serious, insanity ascribing intentions. But when we *are* in the business of making a serious insanity ascription, we are usually aware of the necessity to distinguish between *this* case and ordinary beliefs and actions that are similar in some ways, so that the grounds we can cite (however indexical or context embedded) for our particular ascription are such that we feel they could convince any other culturally competent person, *irrespective* of his religious, political or moral convictions. This is not to deny that railroading of political deviants might take place (although I have yet to read of any discovery of such in this country over the past ten years or so). The 1959 Mental Health Act also makes provision for the exception from insanity ascription and hospitalization of 'morally' deficient people (e.g. promiscuous people) because it is apparent that rational life styles can range across the spectrum of moral commitments, and sexual conduct of all kinds finds articulate and rational champions.

For our purposes, the point of interest is that the 'continuum theory of insanity' can only be sustained in disengagement from knowledge of the practical psychiatric operations it purports to depict in some way. It is an idle theory, and a travesty of common sense. Psychiatric personnel, when called upon to justify their ratification of someone's status as mentally disordered (e.g. by a court of law), need to show that they have arrived at their assessment on warrantable grounds, and this involves disentangling the particulars of the case from any superficially similar analogues in normal and mundane living. If there are categories of non-psychotic conduct closely approximating to the 'symptom' thought decisively characteristic of someone labelled as mentally ill, then it becomes a relevant issue for the psychiatrist that he demonstrate the distinctive and peculiar character of the belief and conduct of the patient which formally resembles the non-psychotic variant. In his book on the Insanity Defence in the District of Columbia, USA,[25] Richard Arens includes a transcript of a case in which a psychiatric consultant is responding to the Defence's question, 'Would you tell us something about that disease process and how it manifests itself?'

*The Witness:*
> ... I might say that in arriving at a conclusion that he has such delusions, I had to make a distinction, which we often have to make, between a person who would be a 'cop hater'—we many times have to examine a patient who has a rather fixed resentment about the police—but because of the very extensive nature of Mr W.'s fears about the police, I have concluded that he has delusions of persecution even at the present time.

The witness went on to specify further the nature of the delusions, and made reference to the person's fears that the jury had been rigged against him by the police, and that when one of the jurors admitted prejudice against him, thereby disqualifying himself from jury service in that trial, Mr W. had taken that as a rigged display, organized by the police, to show that he was the sort of person against whom someone might be prejudiced. This was, then, for all to see, no ordinary case of cop hating, but 'an indication of a profound mental disorder'.[26] It is not clear whether the reference to the cop hater possibility was an attempt to anticipate a possible further question which might have been aimed at undercutting the insanity ascription by mentioning precisely that category of people and including Mr W. within them and, hence, within a sane (albeit extremist) spectrum of eccentricity. It is not clear whether the reference might have been intended to establish what Dorothy Smith has called a 'contrastive structure,'[27] in which someone's conduct is displayed as deviant in contrast even to some *lesser* deviation, or where some norm is displayed as breached by reference to some other conduct which establishes that norm. In either case (both of which are plausible, since both describe states of affairs which do obtain for these kinds of social procedures), the witness has separated out Mr W. from any incorporation into a category of people to whom the application of the label of insanity would be equivocal. The patient, theorized out of any candidature of a sane population, sometimes resorts to drawing attention to the formal resemblances between his beliefs and those of people to whom insanity has not been ascribed, but the onus is upon *him* to do the necessary persuading which could lead to the transformation of his identification by others as one standing outside of membership of such other groups. When such a strategy is adopted by a patient, there are at least signs present that he is engaging in a reflective appraisal of his condition. How far one travels with him is a wholly situational and judgemental matter.

What I have been trying to do in this discussion is to move a little way toward describing the position of the concept of 'delusion' in some of the judgemental operations of people whose use of the concept is part of their routine practical tasks. I have not tried to characterise mental health personnel as working with a wholly exclusive body of knowledge—indeed, wherever appropriate, I have tried to indicate how their operations are tied to common-sense rationalities of judgment and inference. There is clearly a good deal of work to be done in this area and a vast amount of data to be analyzed in these terms. I would argue that there is no way to construct a rigorous sociology of mental illness along other lines.

It might be argued that I have focussed almost exclusively on a set of *rational* psychiatric practices and dealings with the insane, and that much psychiatric activity is irrational. As I have noted, my concern is not with an ethical or political *critique* of practical actions, only their analytic depiction. The data with which I have been concerned was gathered randomly; the materials are open to further analytic specification by whoever is interested to pursue such a task. I am not interested in judging people's performances, or the nature of the tasks they accomplish, and this means that *any* item of action, lay or professional, relating to psychiatric questions, can be of interest as a real world phenomenon. Again, it might be argued that I have ignored certain facts about the institutional structures 'within' which mental health personnel work. But the onus there is on the critic to demonstrate (a) how further contextual considerations could *warrantably* be imported into my analysis and (b) how such considerations would cast light on the very general analytic issues I have been attempting to generate. It is of great importance in this style of work to separate out unexplicated members' assertions about things in the world and their interrelations from analytic statements which seek to show how practical actions and practical reasoning can be seen to work.

## NOTES

1. Alan Blum 'The Sociology of Mental Illness' in Jack D. Douglas (ed.) *Deviance and Respectability. The Social Construction of Moral Meanings* Basic Books (1970) pp. 38-9
2. Harvey Sacks 'Sociological Description' *Berkeley Journal of Sociology* vol. 8 1963 pp. 1-13
3. I have outlined elsewhere the developmental trend in the work of Harold Garfinkel from his early conception of rule-governed conduct to his later preoccupation with the properties of rules and their situational, contingent uses (see 'The Ethnomethodological Programme in Contemporary Sociology,' forthcoming in *The Human Context* 1973). It is especially important that the distinctively ethnomethodological view of rules is understood (and there are many signs that the critics of ethnomethodology are far from such comprehension, many taking the early perspective as the abiding one). The problem of rules is not peculiar to ethnomethodological interests; Wittgenstein's later work can profitably be read as a sustained attempt to grapple with the role of rules in human communication and conduct, and with their various forms. In sociology, there has long been a tendency to pay lip service to 'norms of action,'

whilst leaving it quite unclear how such norms or rules are grounded in everyday courses of action. As soon as one focuses upon that issue, it becomes clear that we are very ignorant of the presuppositions of rule use, and the ways in which rules are used not only to guide conduct but to bring conduct into some scheme of interpretation. Moreover, there are vexed questions about the ways in which an analyst might go about *formulating* rules that members might be claimed to be following. One must avoid treating action-*in-accord-with*-a-rule as action-*governed-by*-a-rule, since one can easily bring some course of observed activity under the auspices of a rule like formulation without such a formulation expressing the state of knowledge of the member doing the activity. James Bogen has commented that, for Wittgenstein's later view of natural language: 'When regularity is needed it does not follow that rules are required to establish it ... rule use turns out to be just another linguistic pactice, no more fundamental or essential than any other to the use of language.' (J. Bogen *Wittgenstein's Philosophy of Language* Routledge & Kegan Paul (1972) p. 190.) For Wittgenstein, the 'background practices' of rule use are the conventions or 'forms of life,' not some further set of rules. Judgmental capacities and regularities in physical comportment would figure amongst 'forms of life'. (For a fuller discussion of this, see J. F. M. Hunter's excellent essay '*Forms of Life* in Wittgenstein's "Philosophical Investigations"' in E. D. Klemke (ed.) *Essays on Wittgenstein* Urbana, University of Illinois Press (1971).) Some recent work in the analysis of the natural logic of practical speech formulates 'rules' of conversation, where a more appropriate claim would be to have formulated 'oriented-to features,' or 'transformable features,' following Sacks's early recommendations. The point is that for members, a recurrent feature of their talk might, given some (uncodifiable) contingencies, be seen as a required feature (rule-ordained), whilst elsewhere merely conventional. The analyst cannot *prescribe* an *invariant* member's orientation irrespective of situational contingencies. But he can, and must, describe *orientable-to features of members' interactional achievements*. A simple example of such a feature would be as follows; in place formulations, members orient to the location of the person to whom the formulation is addressed in such a way as to preclude the production of a formulation that is based on discrepant knowledge. Thus, I would orient to formulating a relevant location in terms familiar to you on the basis of my analysis of your stock of knowledge at hand—if your mother lived at 100 Arcadia Avenue, and I had just visited there, I might produce the utterance 'I've just visited your mother', rather than 'I've just been to 100 Arcadia Avenue', unless I was seeking to produce a joke between us, which could only work given our respective assignments of relevant knowledge as an oriented-to feature of the conversation.

4.   The notions of 'membership categories' and 'membership categorisation devices' belong to Harvey Sacks. I am indebted to Professor Sacks for having made available to my wife and myself a large set of transcripts of his lectures. Much of the work on MCDs is now published.

5.   See Stanley Cavell 'The Availability of Wittgenstein's Later Phil-

osophy in George Pitcher (ed.) *Wittgenstein* Macmillan (1968) pp. 151-85, especially p. 158 & pp. 160-61. Also see Barry Stroud 'Wittgenstein and Logical Necessity' in ibid pp. 477-96, and J. F. M. Hunter op. cit.

6. W. A. White 'The Language of Schizophrenia' *Archives of Neurology and Psychiatry* vol. 16 (1926) pp. 395-413

7. C. J. Raven 'Verbal Dysfunctions in Mental Illness' *Language and Speech* vol. 1 (1958) pp. 218-25

8. M. Lorenz 'Problems Posed By Schizophrenic Language' *Archives of General Psychiatry* vol. 4 (1961) pp. 603-10. See also D. V. Forrest 'Poesis and the Language of Schizophrenia' *Psychiatry* vol. 28, (1965) pp. 1-18

9. W. A. Hunt & F. Arnoff 'The Repeat Reliability of Clinical Judgment of Test Responses' *Journal of Clinical Psychology* vol. 12 (1956) pp. 289-90

10. Harold J. Vetter *Language Behaviour and Psychopathology* Chicago, Rand McNally & Company (1969) p. 160

11. E. Von Domarus 'The Specific Laws of Logic in Schizophrenia' in J. S. Kasanin (ed.) *Language and Thought in Schizophrenia* Berkeley, University of California Press (1944)

12. ibid p. 111 et seq

13. E. F. Kal (letter) in *American Journal of Psychiatry* vol. 125 (1969) p. 1128

14. The term 'jaundice' is often incorrectly used as a disease-term, whereas it refers to the yellowed complexion of a patient suffering from either of the two diseases referred to in parentheses. The term 'schizophrenia' can only rationally be used to refer to conduct, beliefs etc since there is no determinable underlying state or condition of the body to which it could apply. That these distinctions (in the cases of 'jaundice' and 'schizophrenia' respectively) are not always drawn in use by professionals competent in medical and/or psychiatric fields does not mean the distinction is arbitrary. (The example of 'jaundice' was suggested to me by Lena Jayyusi).

15. Ludwig Wittgenstein *On Certainty* (hence: *On C.*) eds. G. E. M. Anscombe and G. H. von Wright, trans. Denis Paul & G. E. M. Anscombe, Oxford, Basil Blackwell, (1969 edition) para. 403

16. *On C.* para. 166. See also paras. 204 & 209 and paras. 143 & 144

17. *On C.* para 160

18. *On C.* para. 154

19. *On C.* para. 257

20. *On C.* para. 378

21. See the essays collected in Bryan R. Wilson (ed.) *Rationality* Oxford, Basil Blackwell (1970)

22. *On C.* paras. 609-612

23. *On C.* para. 279. Wittgenstein remarked elsewhere (*Phil. Investig.* p. 190) that: 'If there were a verb meaning 'to believe falsely,' it would not have any significant first person present indicative.' This amounts to a declaration that it is illogical to suppose that a man could avow his own deluded condition. However, Mats Furberg (in his *Saying and*

*Meaning* Oxford (1971) pp. 232-33) has proposed that one could say that one was the victim of a delusion in the present tense thus: 'I believe falsely that pink elephants are running after me.' I find this wholly muddleheaded. It is obviously possible that a man might claim that he *believed* falsely that *p.,* but a present tense avowal is a contradiction—if one knows that one is deluded, one is no longer deluded.

24.   Bernard Rimland 'Psychogenesis versus Biogenesis: The Issues and the Evidence' in Stanley C. Plog and Robert B. Edgerton (eds.) *Changing Perspectives in Mental Illness* Holt, Rinehart & Winston (1969), pp. 702-35

25.   Richard Arens *Make Mad The Guilty* Springfield, Illinois, U.S.A., Charles C. Thomas. Extract from p. 151

26.   ibid p. 152 (Witness's remark)

27.   Dorothy Smith 'Sub-version of Mental Illness (K Is Mentally Ill)'. Mimeographed paper cited by kind permission of the author.

# CHAPTER FIVE

# Transcultural Psychopathology

Anthropology provides us with a rich source of ethnographic materials on cultural variations which have for some years embarrassed proponents of the view that psychiatric theories of human nature are universal in scope. Moreover, there are many who concur with Marvin Opler's assertion that:

> Those who claim that schizophrenias (of modern type) are biogenetic in origin and therefore distributed randomly in populations are simply ignorant of the anthropological data. Variations in the form and epidemiology of mental illnesses occur transculturally.[1]

Opler's is an uncompromising view. He states that modes of 'hysteriform behaviour' occur in peasant societies (including the more differentiated Javanese society) and that: 'such illnesses are quite different from the schizophrenias with paranoid reactions encountered so frequently in modern European and American society'.[2] Ari Kiev has contributed further notes on modes of conduct and judgmental styles characteristic of people diagnosed in non-Western cultures as mentally disordered, and he discusses the existence of 'exotic psychoses' which defy incorporation into Western psychiatric gnosology: the Malayan *amok,* the Witiko psychoses of the Cree, Salteaux and Ojibwa, the Arctic *pibloktoq,* the Malayan *latah,* the *imu* illness of Hokkaido and the Chinese *koro.*[3] Kiev has also drawn attention to the cross-cultural divergences in what are claimed indigenously to constitute the characteristic 'symptomatologies' of schizophrenic patients: catatonic rigidity, negativism and stereotypy for India, aggressiveness and expressiveness for Southern Italy, and quietude for most Africans.[4] Alexander Leighton consulted informants amongst the Yoruba of Nigeria and concluded that, whilst Yoruba healers regarded most of the symptom patterns of Western psychiatric gnosology either as signs of trouble, undesirable conduct or illness :

> Three exceptions to this generalisation were ... encountered. Our informants were not acquainted with either phobic or obsessive compulsive symptom patterns. Depression as a unified pattern was also unfamiliar. We detected no indication that the Yoruba are familiar with symptom patterns that are unfamiliar to psychiatry. But their concepts and typology of causes are in a framework so different from that of psychiatry as to make comparisons largely impossible.[5]

Leighton's study is methodologically suspect in several ways; we are not told whether the Yoruba informants were simply questioned about their views in the abstract, or whether they were observed over time in practical engagements with people, and we are not told how representative his informants could be claimed to be of Yoruba healers in general. Nonetheless, it is clear that his research is but one part of a considerable literature on small cultures replete with ethnopsychiatric schemes alien to Western psychiatric relevences.

If it is the case that many disorders recognized as mental illness in alien cultures cannot fit into the classificatory schemes worked out in Western psychiatry, it is also the case that many of the presentations of people diagnosed as schizophrenic etc in *our* culture formally resemble those of people thought quite sane, rational and rule-following in other cultural environments. The Englishman who believes that his head is kept in a box that he carries about could well be a candidate for mental hospitalization, but certain Yoruba are reported to

> ... carry about with them boxes covered with cowrie shells, which they treat with special regard. When asked what they are doing, they apparently reply that the boxes are their heads or souls and that they are protecting them against witchcraft.[6]

Of course, this formal resemblance does not make the Englishman's belief any less a delusion, any less insane. There are culturally available grounds amongst the Yoruba for believing the above; there are no such grounds in England. Sometimes, an illicit post hoc contextual transposition is attempted by those who would wish us to see conduct and belief, assessed as mad in the contexts in which it was observed, torn out of those contexts and assessed against broader considerations such as the existence of co-believers and whole normative orders conducive to such beliefs and such conduct elsewhere in the world. This is similar to Laing's already noted attempt to construct hypothetical contexts (of deranged family interactions) against which to assess beliefs and modes of conduct. One can, of course, always construct contexts within which *any* beliefs and conduct can be seen as rule-following or strategically constructed and so forth; the point about insanity-ascribing procedures which I have tried to establish is that they are generally wholly sensitive to seeing the relevant conduct and belief in terms of some notions of adequate performance in the contexts and culture within which they were found, since those contexts and cultural milieux furnish the very resources that are employed in conceptualizing the beliefs and conduct in the first place as inappropriate and groundless. The Haitian voodoo believer who reports holding conversations with the dead, and the Yoruba who 'carry their heads around,' could both be envisaged doing the same thing in this country; it is obvious that their beliefs and conduct would be assessed in the light of the normative order of their own cultures and not in the light of ours so that no one would sanctionably consider them insane (unless they considered the original cultures 'insane'). In other words, whilst it is true that insanity ascriptions are cultu. sensitive, no insanity ascriber could take as an excusing condition for some mad belief held by an Englishman in England the 'explanation' that he happens to believe the same things believed by some Haitians or Yoruba. The beliefs are mad because the Englishman has no possible source of social corroboration of his beliefs *where he avows them*. Beliefs and conduct are never appraised by any competent person in pure abstraction; what is appraised is belief and conduct in context. The only relevant context for the appraisal of beliefs is the knowledge people have of the culture and circumstances in which they are avowed and seen as problematic.

In my discussion of delusions, I tried to show that the beliefs we have depend upon our styles of judgment, and that disjunctions in styles of judgment underpin the ascriptions of delusions. It is clear that styles of judgment differ in certain respects transculturally (although not so much as to prohibit the possibility of translation and cross-cultural understandings). There is in anthropology a good deal of literature which is often referred to as 'culture and personality' writings; this literature features descriptions of 'modal personality types' of different cultures and seeks to relate characterological data to descriptions of 'cultural environment' (often on the

model of relating biological data to ecological environment—
unfortunately). What such descriptions of 'modal types' amount to
is often a set of accounts of common judgmental styles found amongst
a people, coupled with more superficial and rashly generalised
reifications of 'personality'. Some anthropologists in this school
frame their observations using psychiatric terminology. Ruth
Benedict describes the Kwakiutl Indian modal personality as
'megalomaniac paranoid,'[7] and notes the proliferation of accepted
'ideas of grandeur' amongst the people. Bateson and Mead[8] portray
the Balinese as 'schizoid' and dissociative, and Young[9] added in his
later assessment that: 'We may find certain parallels (with them)
among our own dementia praecox patients.' Fortune,[10] writing on
the Dobuans, notes their 'paranoid' personality type, their regular
and institutionalised ideas of persecution, hostility and suspicion.
Erikson,[11] describing the Yurok, observes that they cry out to
their gods 'like babies' and hallucinate in their meditations 'like
psychotics'. As generalised descriptions and evaluations, these
remarks are wholly ethnocentric—in Wallace's terms

> . . . a society of psychotics is a contradiction in terms, and the use
> of a diagnostic label in national character evaluations expresses
> merely the author's hostility toward the subject of his description.[12]

This is not to claim that the evaluations made by these writers
are only idiosyncratic. They probably express views that many
Western visitors to these cultures would accept. What is distasteful
about them is the fact that they are proffered as anthropological
findings, whereas their status is that of members' observations. There
is no reason why the anthropologist should engage in the kind of
assessments that anyone could make of a whole culture; this is
neither distinctive nor revelatory in its contribution. On the other
hand, this is not to suggest that alien cultures must remain closed
to criticism from without, insulated from all but their own self-
assessments. The issue here is that such assessments, whilst they
should not be blind to the peculiarities of local conditions described
by the anthropologist, are the concerns of *any* member and not the
province of expert specialism. Leaving that argument aside, it
becomes apparent that observations of alien cultural conventions
of the sort isolated above do have implications for those who would
suggest that it is possible to define universal 'norms' of 'mental
health' or pan-human 'psychological' attributes relevant to the
assessment of any individual anywhere in terms of his 'sanity'.

Two theorists, Paul Halmos[13] and Andrew Crowcroft,[14] maintain that it is possible to define absolute norms *and* abnorms of human functioning. Halmos refers to the existence of what he calls 'bio-psychological potentialities' of human beings that constitute 'the ontological basis of the pan-human norm'.[15] He asserts that these 'bio-psychological' potentials 'must be culturally uncontaminated'.[16] Since a 'culturally uncontaminated' type is simply a behaving organism of some kind, one is left wondering what this could amount to. We cannot speak sensibly of precultural or acultural 'psychological' features at all; conscious mental functioning *derives from* acculturation. Human sounds and movements gain their sense as characteristics of human conduct only in terms of cultural conventions. Halmos is clearly searching for some non-evaluative specification of mental health and mental abnormality with his conceptions of 'bio-psychological' tendencies and 'ontological bases,' but it is a fruitless search. Our judgments about people in psychiatric terms cannot be underpinned in this manner. There is no reason to suppose that, because we cannot state a generalised description of conduct which any competent member of any human culture would construe as an account of abnormal functioning (given contextual supplementation describing settings), therefore our culturally specific assessments are in some sense unfounded. Crowcroft takes up some of Halmos' points quite avidly; as a psychiatrist concerned to defend the 'objectivity' of his work, he argues against what he calls the 'cultural relativist thesis' and in favour of two main propositions. These are : (1) there are absolute psychoses, and (2) conforming individuals in 'abnormal cultures' (the Yurok and Dobuans are cited as such) are in fact abnormal in an absolute sense, despite finding complete acceptance within their own cultural milieux.[17] The conception of an 'absolute psychosis' is unclear; as I have already suggested, there is no reason to doubt that some people are unequivocally insane even if their conduct and belief(s) formally resemble those of members of alien cultures. Disjunctions in transcultural diagnostic schedules also worry Crowcroft, and he reacts by postulating a unilateral set of condemnatory judgments against the 'psychological health' of whole societies with whose cultural conventions and moral codes he disagrees, as if this in some way resolves the disjunctions. The problem is, why construe such disjunctions in abstract standards as embarrassments for psychiatry in the first place? Any practical psychiatric work is intelligible only against the background of the cultural conventions within which it operates, and cultural conventions do indeed differ. Extrapolating common denominators from transcultural materials and reifying one's own standards as ontological absolutes will not remedy this situation, if it stands in need of remedial attention in the first place. This entire exercise appears to stem from misconceiving *psychiatry*, as distinct from psychopathology, as a theoretical, scientific enterprise with respect to which questions about objectivity could legitimately be raised. Actually, psychiatric practices are unavoidably and essentially bound up with the pragmatics of everyday living, and the objectivity of psychiatric judgements is more a matter of reasonableness and necessary precautions in specific cases than of operating according to universal, culture-neutral principles and procedures. Every diagnostic procedure shorn of reference to cultural conventions and standards of conduct is irrelevant to the central, practical concerns of psychiatry; this is why Joseph Zubin's work on responses to electrical stimulation, reaction times and so forth with 'schizophrenics',[18] undertaken in order to determine 'culture free' diagnostic standards, is unlikely ever to prove relevant to practitioners and could not logically preclude the prior, culturally founded recognition process that generates our 'schizophrenics' in the first place. But this is no cause for lamentation; the idea of a psychiatry without cultural reference is like the idea of conceptual thought without language—in both cases, the latter is partially constitutive of the former, and could in no sense be considered a *fetter* upon it. We should not be so readily tempted into harbouring a common view that sees ordinary cultural knowledge as always defective; commonsense cultural knowledge and standards are not all of a piece, but are accomodated to particular sorts of work, and enable us to do that work (the tasks of psychological assessments amongst others) adequately and routinely. Attempts to replace the pragmatics and ad hoc features of mundane psychiatric practice by substituting sharp, context free procedural canons must inevitably produce artificial and arbitrary courses of action in which there is no room for the exercise of situated judgments and contextual considerations. Just as Wittgenstein noted that we cannot construe common speech as formulable in a calculus, neither can we construe psychiatry and psychological assessments as rigidly rule-governed (even though we can discern the operation of conventional procedures and presuppositions in both).

## NOTES

1. Marvin K. Opler 'Anthropological Contributions to Psychiatry and Social Psychiatry' in Stanley C. Plog & Robert B. Edgerton (eds.) *Changing Perspectives in Mental Illness* Holt, Rinehart & Winston (1969) p. 102

2. ibid p. 103

3. Ari Kiev 'Transcultural Psychiatry: Research Problems and Perspectives' in Plog & Edgerton (eds.) op. cit. pp. 106-27

4. ibid p. 116

5. Alexander H. Leighton 'A Comparative Study of Psychiatric Disorders in Nigeria and Rural North America' in Plog & Edgerton (eds.) op. cit. p. 196. See also his collaborative work with T. A. Lambo, C. C. Hughes, D. C. Leighton, J. M. Murphy and D. P. Macklin *Psychiatric Disorder among the Yoruba* New York, Cornell University Press (1963)

6. Martin Hollis 'Reason and Ritual' in Bryan R. Wilson (ed.) *Rationality* Oxford, Basil Blackwell (1970) p. 221

7. Ruth Benedict *Patterns of Culture* Boston, Houghton Mifflin (1934)

8. G. Bateson & M. Mead *Balinese Character: A Photographic Analysis* New York, Special Publications of the New York Academy of Sciences, 11 (1942)

9. Kimball Young *Handbook of Social Psychology* (1946) p. 56

10. R. F. Fortune *The Sorcerers of Dobu* New York, Dutton (1932)

11. E. H. Erikson *Childhood and Society* New York, W. W. Norton (1963) p. 157

12. A. F. C. Wallace 'Culture Change and Mental Illness' in Plog & Edgerton (eds.) op. cit. p. 81

13. Paul Halmos *Towards a Measure of Man* London, Routledge & Kegan Paul (1957)

14. Andrew Crowcroft *The Psychotic. Understanding Madness* Penguin (1968)

15. Halmos op. cit. p. 48

16. ibid p. 49

17. A. Crowcroft op. cit. pp. 55-6

18. J. Zubin 'A Cross-Cultural Approach to Psychopathology and Its Implications for Diagnostic Classification' in L. D. Eron (ed.) *The Classification of Behaviour Disorders* Chicago (1966) pp. 43-82

# Conclusion:
# Cognition as a Moral Order

If the arguments sketched in the preceding chapters are adequate, they point to a programme of work radically distinct from traditional inquiries undertaken in sociology and social psychology into mental illness. Usually, discussions about psychopathology that stress the normative ordering of judgments and procedures involved in dealing with mental disorders tend to collapse into despair or debates about remedial, value-purging methods of 'objective' investigation into causes and rates. The alternative, given a little substance in my discussion of insanity ascription, would be to focus upon the *conventional procedures and presuppositions* involved in *any* set of recorded instances of talk about psychological status. We are still without rigorous descriptions of the routine, conventional methods by which members of a culture go about construing the cultural competence of others, although some work in this area is beginning to emerge, within the paradigm developed by Harold Garfinkel—'ethnomethodology'.[1] Garfinkel's work on practical reasoning and commonsense procedures for constructing communicative interaction in everyday life has been developed in the area of inferential and categorization procedures by Harvey Sacks in a series of brilliant papers,[2] and there is great promise in this work for studies of insanity as a socially assembled phenomenon.

However, I doubt very much that work undertaken along such lines could remain confined to the immediate area of insanity research; the remarks that I have been able to make suggest that there are many directions along which one might travel, having begun to deal rigorously with cognition as a socially structured and normatively ordered phenomenon. I want to take up one or two points raised by Peter McHugh in a paper called 'A Commonsense Perception of Deviance'[3] in order to exemplify the interrelationship of deviancy theorizing and a concern for cognition as a moral order.

McHugh argues that for members of American culture (and it is clear that what he says holds good for British culture), there are two practical concerns that have to be addressed before an act can be accorded the status of 'deviant'. Firstly, the agent of the act in question must be seen to have acted *conventionally,* which, in McHugh's terminology, means that his act must be seen to have been performed in a situation where it is conceived that *alternatives* were available to him. Secondly, the agent of the act in question must be seen to have acted *theoretically,* which means that the agent must be in a position where it makes sense to ascribe *relevant knowledge* of the circumstances and what he was doing in them to that agent. McHugh then moves on to differentiate out the ascription of knowledge by familiarity and ad hoc practical knowledge (of the sort we might ascribe to children faced with a task of self-presentation in e.g. interviews) from theoretical or *formulable* knowledge. The latter is relevant to deviancy assessments. Non-conventional conduct is coerced, accidental or miraculous; non-theoretical conduct is standardized, habitual and non-formulated (or formulable) by actors. I have already noted that there are divergencies amongst member formulations of insanity along the conventional/nonconventional dimension, but members (if not some phenomenological theoreticians) are agreed that for practical purposes the actors to whom they are seriously ascribing insanity are non-theoretical actors. Sometimes it is considered by members that a child has become insane due to coercion (organic theorizing) or accident (again, biological or hereditary accident) or both (the insanity arising out of the biological causation that in turn is attributable to heredity or, more commonly, bad luck). When members' offspring are not the agents in question, there is sometimes more laxity about assessments of conventionality—poor biographical experiences are more admissible for ascription to a stranger than to one's own son, daughter or spouse on the grounds that one's own responsibilities are implicated in the latter cases. McHugh himself is non-committal about madness in terms of his schema, but he notes that, whatever the 'mix' or permutation of the dimensions thought appropriate for the assessment of the insane, each 'mix' (theoretical/non-conventional, non-theoretical/conventional, etc) has its own consequences.

The attempt to have insanity pleas governed by considerations of conventionality, and not solely by theoreticity, has a long history in our legal system. The famous (or notorious) M'Naghten Rules, formulated in 1843 by the Law Lords, established three broad considerations which had to be entertained before mental abnormality could be established as a defence to a criminal charge : (i) the accused, at the time of his act, must have suffered from a defect of reason, (ii) this must have resulted from a 'disease of the mind', and (iii) the upshot must have been that the accused did not know the nature of his act or that it was illegal.[4] H. L. A. Hart, writing on the history and philosophy of law, noted in connection with these rules that critics concentrated their attack upon rule (iii), arguing that it amounted to a dogmatic denial of the fact that a man might know what he was doing and that it was wrong or illegal, yet could not control his actions.

> The point just is that in a civilized system only those who *could have* kept the law should be punished. Why else should we bother about a man's knowledge or intention or other mental element except as throwing light on this?[5]

Lord Atkin's Committee recommended in 1923 an addition to the M'Naghten Rules to cater for what it termed 'irresistible impulse' (something then allowed under US law), but this was rejected and it was not until 1957 that the plea of diminished responsibility came into operation. Even then, as Hart remarks, some judges (e.g. Lord Goddard in R. v Spriggs, 1958) refused to direct juries to consider the accused's *capacity to conform to* the law, rather than simply his knowledge of it. Construing types of insanity as non-conventional *in law* became permissible very recently in this country, and was considered a humanitarian move.

Hart has argued elsewhere that our very concept of an 'action' is not descriptive but fundamentally ascriptive in character.[6] It is a 'defeasible' concept, 'to be defined through exceptions and not by a set of necessary and sufficient conditions whether physical or psychological'.[7] To say 'Smith did it,' or 'Smith hit her' under normal circumstances of practical engagement amounts to an ascription of liability. Smith was the agent responsible for the hitting. Smith can then deny the charge by denying the facts on which it is based, or he can attempt to 'reduce' it by adding riders such as 'accidentally', 'inadvertently', 'by mistake for someone else' 'in self-defence,' 'under provocation,' 'under threat' or 'by reason of temporary insanity'. In each case, there are different self-ascriptions of relevant knowledge operating. McHugh makes reference (indirectly) to the defeasibility of the morality of action when he notes that a failure to do what is required by a moral rule can only be construed by others as a deviant act in the absence of the relevant conditions of failure to conform.[8] Ingenuity in getting out of an ascription of deviance can consist in constructing a 'relevant condition of failure' not considered by, or unknown to, the deviance ascribing observer(s). Deviance is not always construed as *defiance* of a rule, convention or expectation, since ascriptions of defiance depend upon ascriptions of relevant knowledge that are not always pertinent to rule violations. This is one reason for the lack of fit between the concept of insanity and the concept of defiance; insanity cannot amount to sustained defiance because knowledge and personal responsibility are not sensibly attributed to insane members. We may start out by conceiving of someone as acting in defiance of moral rules and conventions of conduct, where no excuses, apologies and mitigating circumstances are articulated by the member in question, but if we come to believe that the defiance lacks motivation in intelligible terms we need to transform our initial ascription to one of insanity. Unmotivated defiance is not the kind of ascription one can sustain across cases for adult members, but in the case of children it is often plausible. This creates problems in deciding when a child's conduct requires psychiatric attention and when it doesn't. Notice that we are making constant reference to cognitive elements such as knowledge, intention, motive and responsibility. These are 'cognitive', not in the old psychological sense of the psychic storehouse, but in the sociological sense of 'relevantly ascribable properties' of members' awareness and outlook.

We are frequently engaged in the methodical specification of people's minds. We can accomplish this work for practical purposes because we are equipped with conventional inferential procedures. Psychiatrists are able to do the work they do with social approval only because their intuitive equipment is put to use in organised ways along the same lines as that of lay members of the culture; there is perhaps greater latitude for speculation and socially sanctioned 'expert insights' for psychiatrists, but there are still limits. Two examples will perhaps illustrate this; in the first case, the psychiatrist is being 'pulled up' for an apparent transgression of 'what everybody knows,' where the person entitled to do this is someone also of professional status—a lawyer; and where the setting facilitates a degree of licensed pedantry—a court of law. The second case illustrates the way in which a psychiatrist can sometimes pass off a judgment, arrived at on extra-psychiatric, moral grounds, as a psychiatric judgment.

*Witness:* My opinion is that most psychiatrists—very many psychiatrists, and particularly my colleagues—do think that people who act out against society are sick, and —
*Court:* What is that again? Everybody that commits a crime is mentally sick?
*Witness:* Is sick, yes.
*Court:* Do you believe that?
*Witness:* Yes.
*Court:* You don't believe in free will, then?
*Witness:* I don't know what it is.
*Court:* You don't know what free will is?
*Witness:* What do you mean by that?
*Court:* Don't you understand what free will is? You are a psychiatrist and you don't know what I mean when I say free will?
*Witness:* No, I don't.[9]

The court, faced with a psychiatric witness giving expert testimony, finds that a particular type of assimilation is being worked by that witness—the incorporation of legally and morally responsible acts of criminality into a medical definition (having done a transformation on . . . 'people who act out against society are sick,' to get : 'Everybody that commits a crime is mentally sick?'). Having made the witness concur to the transformation (or assertion of implication) of his utterance, the court again checks that this implication is sustained by the witness, thus binding him to it. Then yet another implication of that position is drawn out and proposed as a corrolary question to the witness ('You don't believe in free will, then?'). The witness then opts for a response that could elicit some specification of the notion 'free will,' but the Court treats this as an occasion, not for a specification, but for a counter question which contains a strong element of mock astonishment which is reiterated in response to the straight request by the witness for the court to state what it means by 'free will'. The issue here seems to revolve around the Court's attempt to sustain a common-sense use of 'free will' to suggest that the 'expert's' self-confessed 'ignorance' is absurd, whereas the psychiatrist might be seen to be orienting toward a *technical* specification which he can then cash in on. The witness's first 'I don't know what it is' response to the question about free will constitutes a denial which is treated as absurd by the Court in the declaration : 'You are a psychiatrist and you don't know . . . .' The contrastive device[10] here turns on the juxtaposition of the category of 'member competent in matters psychological' with the ascription of 'ignorance of matters psychological,' but this only works if the hearer (jury, judge, etc) sustains the primacy of commonsense psychological knowledge over and above any modifications which the psychiatrist may have in mind. It is also interesting to note the proliferation of authoritative sources cited by the witness at the outset of his remarks ('most psychiatrists —very many psychiatrists, and particularly my colleagues . . .'), against which any opponent of his version must contend. This piece of data also raises some interesting issues about the discourse generating properties of 'enthymematic' statements—statements that do not express the grounds on which their propositions rest. When a member elaborates some proposition, he can do so in his identity as someone expert on the topic, or as a commonsense person; where the topic being discussed is treatable within either a technical or a commonsense framework, problems of procedurally relevant treatment can arise when the appropriate frame is not made explicit. Sometimes, such a 'problem' can be created deliberately in the anticipation of bringing off a strong contrast between 'expert talk' and 'ordinary talk' about the topic. One can say : 'Oh, but I thought we were talking about X in a technical sense—I didn't realise you had taken it at *that* level,' and thereby achieve an illustration of the truncated, partial or distorted character of the lay, commonsense version; and one might also be in a position to manage a conversation in such a way that the technical orientation of one speaker is treatable as pedantry. This latter seeems to me attributable intuitively to the extract before us, where the court is so managing the interaction (due to the rules of court procedure) to deflate the technical version of the psychiatrist.

The second instance of latitude in the exercise of psychiatric judgment in courts of law is furnished by A. K. Daniels.[11] She cites the self-description of the tactics used by an ex Air Force psychiatrist in dealing with a man who, in the course of delivering cargo overseas, got drunk, and made a homosexual advance toward another member of his crew :

I was called to give expert testimony. They wanted to know whether or not he was a homosexual. In my heart, I thought he was; but didn't take that position . . . what I did say was impossible to attack. I pointed out the vast quantity of alchohol the man had consumed. Enough to knock a man flat. I pointed out that a man coming out of anaesthesia behaves in a way not regular (or usual). (And I managed to get him off.)[12]

In spite of the edited nature of this data, we can still see how a psychiatrist can use his authority in order to mask a moral judgment of someone's best interests by articulating a plausible, commonsense version of his situation. The central point here is that even a psychiatrist must provide a case for his version that is congruent with commonsense knowledge. Homosexuality is an indefeasible status— once an episode of a homosexual advance has occurred, the person responsible *is* a homosexual irrespective of the non-occurrence of further advances. Only a carefully advertised redefinition of himself (which may even involve 'recognising' that he was, all along, really a homosexual) can purge the attributed status. This accounts for the trial on the basis of one incident. The only way to redefine the man's status, if one wanted to do so (as this psychiatrist did), is to show that the man's conduct is wholly attributable to loss of control—i.e. to postulate a non-conventional version in McHugh's terms. Relying upon the indeterminacy of our knowledge of severe alcoholic effects, the psychiatrist was able to 'blame it on the beer'. Moreover, the severity of the alcoholic effects is important; the less the quantities consumed, the less the drunkenness, the more the man might be thought merely to have lost his 'normal inhibitions' and to have revealed his *real* character, his covert or underlying homosexuality. I have shown earlier the sort of interactional work that can be done with the notions of 'covert' hallucinatory experiences and the like. Not every status can intelligibly be seen as dichotomized into 'overt' and 'covert', and this is an area in which some work could profitably be undertaken.

I want to turn at this point to address myself to some methodological issues. It is clear that the methodological approach recommended in this work is radically different from that which consists in specifying causal or quasi-causal connections between operationalized variables ('schizophrenia' and 'social class,' 'mental disorder' and 'social integration,' 'insanity' and 'maritally schismatic family structure,' etc). The approach encouraged here is tied up with the task of analytical description of members' practices. It is assumed that for any situated utterances there can be given more than one 'correct' or 'adequate' reading. The problem is not to arrive at some stipulative criterion for deciding between readings, but to set out some commonsense readings and show how they could be accounted for in terms of the use of conventional cultural procedures and presuppositions. This permits insights into the organization of cultural knowledge and the rich methodicity of everyday interactional accomplishments. One is not required to claim, with Aaron Cicourel, that our interest lies in stating the ways in which an actor in everyday life uses grammar, intonations, kinesic and ecological information in settings to generate his interpretation of the social environment;[13] rather, it is a more modest and accurate claim that we seek out and state the logically unavoidable procedures and presuppositions informing the utterances and interpretations which members *can* make, irrespective of guessing any situated reading a member *does* make. Our interest lies not in definitive warrants for interpretations, but in specifying available interpretive procedures. Cicourel's complaint about lack of information on uses of grammar, kinesics and so on, which he hopes will be remedied by sociolinguistic and ethnomethodological inquiries,[14] relates to his style of work; he is not so much concerned with the analytical description of members' conventional procedures as a problem on its own, but seems to call for specifications usable in field work research on e.g. particular settings such as police bureaux. This demands that the sort of information he requires be employed in making inferences about 'what is happening here,' 'what X is really doing' and the like. For this reason, he also requires models of actor-relevances.[15] The sort of propositions found in the work of ethnomethodologists such as Sacks, Schegloff, Jefferson, Turner and others[16] relates not to the provision of context free inferential and imputational criteria (e.g. the provision of the essential features of an insult, joke, story or whatever which could enable a researcher to read off such phenomena mechanically from other data), but to the provision of abstract accounts of members' manifold but orderly ways of accomplishing communication. For Cicourel, the emphasis is upon the researcher's having to make 'explicit remarks as to the meaning of the communication exchanges'[17] he encounters between the people he studies. For most other ethnomethodologists, the emphasis is upon analyzing the formal procedures and background cultural knowledge informing a given reading, whether or not *that* reading was the one employed by the members whose communicative exchanges constitute the data for analysis. Such analyses aim *at the highest level of abstraction and generality,* whilst Cicourel remains at the level of warranting a specific reading, or account of the 'meaning' of his data : moreover,

> ... in analyzing conversations and reports, the researcher must approximate a "rewriting" of the dialogue or prose so that he can communicate the unstated and seen but unnoticed background expectancies for the reader. Such a procedure would enable the reader to understand how the participants and observer made sense of their environments as portrayed by the researcher.[18]

I think this clearly articulates Circourel's position (of 1968). It involves rendering explicit the guesswork of the researcher in arriving at his portrayals; conversations and reports are not analysed for their most general properties, but for purposes of (re)constructing situational and indexical (context specific) relevances which might be assumed to have gone into their original production. The rewriting remains, in Cicourel's own terms, measurement by fiat,[19] or constructivist analysis. It is the easiest possible trap for the sociologist attracted by the ethnomethodological programme to suppose that such work can be used to underpin particular accounts of social situations, communicative exchanges and other surface phenomena. The participant observer inquiring into the social organisation of some institution, residential area or factory is doing the sort of sociology for which remedies are not forthcoming. Ethnomethodology announces no less than a paradigm shift; a complete reformulation of what is to count as data, researchable problems and findings; it is incommensuraté with a substantive topic orientation to social research. There is, for instance, no reason to suppose that we can obtain fuller knowledge of the conventional procedures used in ascriptions of deviance solely by focussing on the work of social control agents in the community. Further, if such a focus is adopted in research, there may be a tendency to impute the stock of procedures analysed to the particular members of some particular collectivity, rather than to the broader domain of cultural competence, without proper heed to the issue of the anonymity and conventionality of the methods described. In other words, one may end up attributing a set of procedural regularities exclusively to some category of societal members (lawyers, psychiatrists, police officers, teachers, parents etc) when in fact one should be aiming at the description of Anyman's conventional methods—the problem with the more circumscribed attributions is that they remain indeterminate and intermeshed with too many contextual details, hunches about situational tactics and speculations about localized knowledge and relevances. (I must leave it to the reader to check my own analytical depictions for their possible faults along these lines; suffice to say that such a check might reveal still further possibilities for more insightful and abstract formulations.)

I do not want to conclude by attempting a summary of my arguments. Such a summary would no doubt compound the repetition already present. I should like, however, to stress that I am in no sense oblivious to the need for research which could prove practically useful in helping suffering people. Much of what I have said has purchase at the level of the logic of *theoretical* research programmes, and in no way detracts from the pursuit of psycho-pharmacology and humanitarian psychiatric practice. I am persuaded, however, of the epistemologically critical position of a science of psychopathology which appears inevitably bound up with inappropriate conceptualizations of mental disorders. Such disorders are not open to generic research strategies at the levels described in my section on formal psychopathology. The substitution of woolly-minded and mystical polemics for rational confrontation at the levels of logic and methodology is an unfortunate spin off from that state of affairs. The attempt to counteract that substitution is the only justification I can think of for the many tortuous pages of this book.

## NOTES

1. Harold Garfinkel *Studies in Ethnomethodology* Prentice-Hall (1967) especially chapters 1, 2 and 8

2. Harvey Sacks 'An Initial Investigation of the Usability of Conversational Data for Doing Sociology' in David Sudnow (ed.) *Studies in Social Interaction* Free Press (1972) pp. 31-74. See also H. Sacks 'On the Analyzability of Stories by Children' in Gumperz & Hymes *Directions in Socioliguistics* Holt, Rinehart & Winston (1972), pp. 325-45 and Sacks's mimeographed UCLA lecture notes

3. P. McHugh 'A Commonsense Perception of Deviance' in Hans

Peter Dreitzel (ed.) *Recent Sociology Vol. 2* Macmillan (1970) pp. 152-80. First published in Jack D. Douglas (ed.) *Deviance and Respectability: The Social Construction of Moral Meanings* Basic Books (1970)

4.   This outline was culled from H. L. A. Hart *Punishment and Responsibility: Essays in the Philosophy of Law* Clarendon Press, Oxford (1968) p. 189

5.   H. L. A. Hart ibid

6.   H. L. A. Hart 'The Ascription of Responsibility and Rights' in A. F. N. Flew (ed.) *Logic and Language (First Series)* Basil Blackwell (1960) p. 161

7.   ibid pp. 161-2

8.   Peter McHugh op. cit. p. 159 & p. 162

9.   Data culled from Richard Arens' *Make Mad the Guilty* Springfield Illinois, U.S.A., Charles C. Thomas (1969) p. 166

10.   The notion of a 'contrastive device' is suggested by Dorothy Smith's related notion of 'contrastive structure'. The latter appears in her mimeographed paper 'K Is Mentally Ill' (cited by permission of the author).

11.   Arlene Kaplan Daniels 'The Social Construction of Military Psychiatric Diagnoses' in H. P. Dreitzel (ed.) op. cit. pp. 182-205. Despite the curious amalgam of positivistic style and interactionist interest, this paper contains some excellent illustrative data relevant to my whole discussion here.

12.   ibid p. 202

13.   Aaron Cicourel *The Social Organisation of Juvenile Justice* John Wiley & Sons Inc. (1968) p. 112. An actor may, for example, use a grammatical construction in an idiosyncratic manner, or he may vary his interpretation of some grammatical structure when it arises in different contexts, etc. It is by no means clear that we are necessarily involved in stating how any given actor arrived at any given interpretation at some point in time by means of his use of grammar, kinesics and so forth. It is essential to separate out the indexical, relevance-bound features of members' uses of linguistic and paralinguistic *resources* from the specification of the conventional *procedures available to members* of a culture for generating *various possible* uses and interpretations at more situated and particularistic levels.

14.   E.g.; 'Recent trends in psycholinguistics, componential analysis or ethnoscience or ethnographic semantics, the ethnography of communication, the analysis of conversation, and ethnomethodological studies have sought to provide rules for moving from the actor's experience to verbal and non-verbal communication, and [rules for moving from] an act or event or sequence of events to a description of activities that can be examined independently by other researchers.' ibid p. 5. I do not subscribe to these claims and characterisations, but they clearly fit with an under-labourer conception of the role of ethnomethodological and communication-analytic research.

15.   A. V. Cicourel *Method and Measurement in Sociology* Free Press (1964), p. 61 p. 222

16.    Work by these sociologists can be found in D. Sudnow (ed.) op. cit. and Jack D. Douglas (ed.) *Understanding Everyday Life* Aldine (1970). Mimeographs are also available.

17.    A. V. Cicourel op. cit. (1968) p. 113

18.    ibid p. 18

19.    A. V. Cicourel op. cit. (1964) p. 12 & p. 28. The conception derives from Warren Torgerson *Theory and Method of Scaling* New York, Wiley (1958) pp. 21-2

# Name Index

# Subject Index

*(NOTE:* Terms mentioned throughout text (e.g. *schizophrenia, psychiatry, insanity,* etc.) have been omitted).